Vermont is Always with You

Vermont
is
Always
with You

Marguerite Hurrey Wolf

Drawings by George Daly

THE NEW ENGLAND PRESS, INC.
Shelburne, Vermont

Copyright © 1969 by Marguerite Hurrey Wolf

First New England Press edition, 1983
Library of Congress Catalogue Card Number: 83-62612
ISBN 0-933050-20-8

(Previously published by The Stephen Greene Press, 1969,
Standard Book Number: 8289-0100-7)

Other books by Marguerite Hurrey Wolf:

The Sheep's in the Meadow, Raccoon's in the Corn
How To Be a Doctor's Wife without Really Dying
Seasoned in Vermont

The author and publisher are grateful to the following publications for their permission to use material in this book:

Burlington Free Press, "Out of the Sap Bucket into the Bean Pot," 1963; *Christian Home*, "Give a Tradition for Christmas," Copyright 1962 by Graded Press; *New England Homestead*, "Apres Ski, Le Deluge," December, 1968; "Bring the Children," Summer, 1969; "Do Ladies Drive Trucks?" January, 1968; "My Kingdom for a Horse," May, 1968; "Pumpkins," March, 1968; "The Roaring Twenties," November, 1968; "The Web-Footed Trout Fisherman," June, 1968; "Which Came First, the Chicken or the Egg?" July, 1968; *Vermont Life*, "Apples of My Eye," Fall, 1967; "The Pig's in the Meadow, the Cow's in the Corn," Fall, 1969; *The Rural Vermonter*, "The Walls of Jericho," July, 1967; "Wayne Nealy, Vermonter," May, 1967. The Frost quotation on page 20 is from "In Winter in the Woods Alone" from IN THE CLEARING by Robert Frost. Copyright © 1962 by Robert Frost, reprinted by permission of Holt, Rinehart and Winston, Inc.

The New England Press, Inc.
P. O. Box 575
Shelburne, Vermont 05482

PRINTED IN THE UNITED STATES OF AMERICA

FOR PATTY AND DEBBIE
AND MY SISTER
FRANCES HURREY PHILIPS

Introduction

WE BOUGHT our little farm in Jericho Center, Vermont, in 1948 because Vermont had beckoned to us for some time. We weren't born there. We didn't move there because of a job. But during a month spent in a converted barn in Underhill Center we felt it was the right place for us to balance our winter city life. My husband was practicing medicine in New York City and we yearned for closer communion with changing seasons and unchanging values. We also thought, after twelve years in apartments, that it would be nice to hammer a nail, dance a jig or plant a radish without getting permission in triplicate from the Supreme Court.

Four years after we bought and summered on our farm, George was asked to be Dean of the University of Vermont College of Medicine and we happily moved north to become "year-round summer folk." We were not Vermonters because we were still "from away," but shortly after my first book, *Anything Can Happen in Vermont*, came out I learned that my ancestors had lived in Brattleboro, Vermont for a hundred years. So the strong sense of returning home was not just wishful thinking but a birthright. It was with great pride that our daughters, Patty and Debbie and I were publicly acknowledged as Vermonters. George had done very creditably in earning rather than inheriting his passage into the inner sanctum.

The house in Jericho Center and especially the do-it-George's-self plumbing was not suitable for winter use, so we bought a post-Revolutionary house in South Burlington and lived there for nine years, shuttling our animals and our lares and penates the seventeen miles to Jericho Center as soon as the girls skipped down the lane on the last day of school in June and back again when the first maple leaf drifted down to rest gently on the surface of our pool. When George was asked how much we farmed he always said, "As much as my wife's back can stand." Fortunately my back and I were younger then and bent easily to the hoe, the pitchfork and the winter winds. Then George's work took him to Boston and we reluctantly sold the house in South Burlington, bequeathing the ghosts of the first owners, who had left us a legacy of their letters in the attic, to Molly and Stewart Agras. We reversed the pattern of our Vermont ancestors who had migrated from Massachusetts to Vermont. Five years later George became Dean of the Medical College at the University of Kansas and like other pioneer Vermonters, a hundred years ago, we headed west with all our worldly goods except of course the little farm in Jericho Center. That will never be for sale. It is the one constant in our changing lives, and all four of us returned there with delight each summer and whenever we could scratch up either the excuse or the money.

It was far harder to leave Vermont for Boston than to leave Boston for Kansas, because my parents had come from the Middle West and I was brought up to believe that that is where the real people are to be found. Now I know why they felt the real people were in the Middle West. The early Kansans were Yankees and brought with them the same spirit of independence and freedom to shape their lives as they saw fit. So, of course, we liked Kansas and the Kansans. Kansas is young enough to welcome change and strangers from "back east." One may qualify as a Kansan in less than a hundred years. It is much more beautiful, hilly and green than New Englanders expect. But then, New Englanders are much more warm-hearted and friendly than Kansans expect. Yes, Kansas is hot in the summer and yes, Vermont is cold in the winter, but if either has a real fault it is that they are fifteen hundred miles apart.

The delightful fact is, and that is what this book is about, that people and animals and their spontaneous reaction to each other and their environment are more alike than different in Shawnee

Mission and Jericho Center. Funny or brave without intending to be, generous and kind because that is the natural way to be; their unselfconsciousness heightens the humor and the dignity of life. It happens in Kansas, or Vermont or, for that matter, any place where one person, or preferably two, responds to the first frost by stirring a batch of apple butter in an iron kettle all day outdoors, or walking up a country road to pop a few milkweed pods and watch the tiny gossamer kites rise and drift and rise again until they are consumed by the conflagration of October.

Contents

Out of Sight, Out of Mind   1

House by the Side of the Road   3

Bring the Children   7

Don't Call the Plumber   10

The Walls of Jericho   14

Easter Means Another Chance   19

Pumpkins   22

O Death, Where Is Thy Sting?   26

Lares and Penates   29

The Pig's in the Meadow, the Cow's in the Corn   34

A Place for Everything   38

Who's Afraid of the Big Bad Sow?   43

The Apples of My Eye   47

A Burden of a Beast   53

Which Came First, the Chicken or the Egg?   59

Do Ladies Drive Trucks?   65

School Buses   70

Wayne Nealy, Vermonter   73

Diana the Huntress   77

Give a Tradition for Christmas   81

Out of the Sap Bucket into the Bean Pot   85

In the Still of the Night   87

Rites of Spring	91
The Web-Footed Trout Fisherman	95
A Vermonter in Kansas	98
On Looking a Gift House in the Mouth	102
Manna from Heaven	107
Apres Ski, Le Deluge	110
Contrary to Nature	115
Vermont is Always with You	117

Vermont is Always with You

Out of Sight,
Out of Mind

WHEN SOMEONE asks you where you were born, do you answer the name of the state or the name of the town? My guess is that if you were born in Vermont you give the name of the town, no matter how small. The same is true in Kansas, and perhaps in some other states with which I am less familiar. In both cases you assume the asker *knows* you are a Vermonter or a Kansan and just wants to know what part of the state you hail from. But if you were born in New Jersey as I was, or on Manhattan Island as our daughters were, you always say the town or city. I don't feel any allegiance to the State of New Jersey so I identify my birthplace by the town, Montclair. Patty and Debbie, like other natives of New York City, don't even think of Manhattan as being a part of New York State.

The fact is that I feel more allegiance to Vermont and Kansas because they make me feel needed to sing their praises and banish false images. There is a state chauvinism in each that I have never felt in New Jersey, New York or Massachusetts. Of course Massachusetts isn't even called a state from within. It's a commonwealth, and what you take pride in there is not where you were born but when your ancestors came over—from England, of course. I'm not saying this through jealousy because one of my own came over not on the *Mayflower* but on the *Speedwell*, which must have been equally elastic and made as many trips as the *Mayflower* to hold all the people whose descendants claim were passengers. I also have an ancestor buried in King's Chapel graveyard in Boston, which is almost as good as a lifetime seat at the Friday Symphony. But I know nothing more than the names of these worthy gentlemen. What I am proud of is my fifth great-grandfather who lived in Brattleboro, Vermont, at the time of the Revolution, and my

1

maternal grandfather who was born in England but came to Wisconsin as a boy, moved west through Iowa to South Dakota which he helped bring into statehood in 1889.

There are other states I am sure that engender this fierce pride. The words, "state-o-Maine" are spoken with reverence in Skowhegan, Wiscasset or East Otisfield, and a Virginian will struggle to contain his indignation if you call him simply a Southerner. He isn't a Southerner. He's a Virginian, just as I think of myself as a Vermonter and an adopted Kansan but not a New Englander or a Mid Westerner.

Often, when we were first in Vermont, it surprised me to hear someone say, "I don't believe there is a finer view in the whole state of Vermont!" Vermont is a small state horizontally because so much of its surface is vertical or nearly so, but this expression seems to encompass the whole world because, to many Vermonters, Vermont *is* the whole world.

When my husband considered a job in New York State, one neighbor was indignant, partly at the thought that George would even consider leaving Vermont, but also because Vermont and New York were enemies two hundred years ago and Vermonters aren't going to forget it in a hurry!

The funniest examples of state pride were shown that summer when we flew back to Vermont from Kansas City for our vacation and rented a Hertz car at the Burlington airport. The car happened to have Maine license plates. Well sir! The first day a neighbor stopped at our little house in the country to see "what out-of-staters were making free with your propitty." The next day we stopped in Richmond and a travelling salesman called out to George, "How are things in Maine?"

"I don't know," George shouted back, "I come from Kansas."

Complete strangers asked us about the price of lobsters, the Aroostook potato crop and marvelled at our ignorance. But we couldn't ignore the smoldering resentment that finally erupted one evening as we stood beside the rented car talking with friends of twenty years in the dooryard of their farm. "Bad enough you went away out there to Kansas to live, but seems if, when you get back for such a short time, the least you could do is see to it that you drive a Vermont car 'stead of one from *out of state!*"

House by the
Side of the Road

WHEN I WAS a little girl I cross-stitched a sampler
with the words, "Let me live in a house by the side of the road and
be a friend to man." It was not a large and intricate sampler like
the one my great-grandmother patiently worked at the age of ten.
Mine was just the outline of a house and tree and two rows of
letters leaning like jack-straws, partly because of my lack of skill,
but mostly because my damp hands made the cloth very resistant.
Having stared at the motto while I laboriously pricked my fingers
and tangled the colored silk, it is a sentiment that is not likely to
slip my mind.

Little did I guess that I was destined to live in two houses by the
side of two different roads, one in Jericho Center, Vermont, and
the other in Mission Hills, Kansas. There have been other houses
and apartments, but they didn't involve me on such close terms
with the passing scene.

We have had the little house in Jericho for thirty-five years, loving it not always wisely but so well that we are likely to keep it until
either it or we collapse. Both parties seem to be nearing that time
with alarming rapidity. It is so near the road, built that way in
1820 for convenience and with Vermont winters in mind, that we
are very much a part of everything that happens on the road. The
country habit of becoming not only aware but curious about every

car, beast or bicycle that passes one's house has become contagious. It is almost a full-time job. You wouldn't expect this much activity on a very minor back road that doesn't lead to any town unless you knew that the artillery range and the Camp Fire Girls' camp are both beyond us. What happens to our tax money is made very clear every Saturday A.M. and every Sunday P.M. in the summer. About fifty large pieces of equipment ranging from artillery guns mounted on trailer trucks to caissons filled with soldiers who delight in greeting our sunbathing daughters in true army fashion, lumber past, sending clouds of dust filtering through our porous walls to settle on the food, the furniture and us.

Then there are the cows that are driven up to pasture each morning and back again each night for milking, clopping along in their disorganized floppy gait and pausing to stare sullenly in our windows. An occasional runaway horse or a questing farm dog varies our passing parade. A fisherman lopes along making a rubbery sound with his waders. Small boys on bicycles drag a foot and leap off, their bicycle wheels still spinning, to ask if they may swim in our pool. But most of these do not require our friendship at the moment. Aside from dispensing an occasional glass of water, confusing directions or the use of our phone, our role is not as active as the sampler indicated. In fact when the children were at the lemonade-stand age, they were frequently dismayed at the indifference of their fellow-man to their fine product.

Oddly enough, the other house, where we lived in the winter, in Mission Hills, Kansas, a residential part of Kansas City, involved us more with those who pass in the night, or day. We lived at the crest of a hill where three streets intersect. Below us was Brush Creek and the fairways of the Kansas City Country Club. One Sunday afternoon in November there was a tentative knocking at the front door and George opened the massive oak portal to find two tiny girls, one very wet and shivering, on the doorstep.

"She fell in the creek," the older one explained, pointing at her vibrating companion. They were ushered into a bathroom. Towels and a blanket and the smallest pair of jeans Patty could find were wedged through a crack in the door, and the spokesgirl ventured out to call her father.

Motorists ran out of gas at our corner. Ladies bumped into each

4

other's fenders and then converged on foot on our house and phone, still blaming each other in their nervousness about their husband's reactions. Delivery truck drivers stormed in angrily to ask where-in-h___" Mission Wood Terrace was. Our street was Mission Drive. Within a mile there was also Mission Road, East Mission

Drive, Mission Wood Road and Mission Wood Terrace, all winding in a scenic but confusing fashion.

In the winter the first snowfall produced instant drama, almost and sometimes actually on our front lawn. Kansas citizens were not accustomed to living with snow. When they stopped on our hill, they gunned their motors, spun their wheels, slid crosswise and then lined up ten or twelve strong in bizarre formation down the hill. It was fun to watch from the warm side of the thermopane when your own car was snug in the garage. But some years ago when the Wescoes lived in this house, their son Bill was about a fifth grader and took the motto on the sampler to heart. He bustled about the kitchen making cocoa and rushed paper cups of it out to the shivering folk in their stalled cars. His mother was watching this heartwarming scene with pride until he dashed back to ask her for change. Change? Never loath to turn a calamity into a killing, Bill was selling the lukewarm home-brew at stadium prices.

But the man on the road is not always aware of the one in the house. We have friends who have a summer home in Greensboro, Vermont. It is a lovely old farmhouse redesigned by its architect owner, Francis Roudebush. The front of the house faces a wide lawn and old-fashioned flower beds, but the side wing of the house, including the master bedroom, is adjacent to a very narrow dirt road. They live in New York City in the winter and Roudy takes particular pleasure in waking on summer mornings to only the twittering of the swallows or the distant click-clack of a combine munching through a field of oats. One summer on the first day of his vacation he woke at dawn, luxuriously aware that no alarm would go off and that he could go back to sleep for several hours. But his reverie was interrupted by a strident voice right outside his window.

"Get up you lazy b_____! Get up before I tan your tails!"

Roudy guiltily leaped out of bed and peering through the curtain saw an elderly farmer, slouched on the seat of his wagon, slapping the reins against the flanks of his reluctant team as they stumbled up the rocky road. The mood was shattered. Roudy still felt the message was for him, and he staggered into his clothes feeling a bit less critical of the taxi drivers and the riveters of Manhattan who hold their peace until at least seven-thirty.

6

Bring the Children

WE DIDN'T TAKE our first family vacation trip in a Conestoga wagon. It just seemed that way. It was about 350 miles from the corner of York Avenue and 70th Street in Manhattan to the corner of the converted barn we had rented in Underhill Center, Vermont, but we spent two nights en route. We thought stopovers would be more relaxing. Hah! It would have been more relaxing to have carried knapsacks on our backs, set up a pup tent and rubbed two sticks together to start a fire.

"Stay overnight with us on the way up and bring the children," urged friends who lived in a charming old house in the Hudson river valley. Besides charm, the house also contained Shaker antiques and equally valuable new wedding presents including Steuben glass goblets displayed on shelves that were on the eye level of our Debbie, an eighteen-month-old toddler. Our hosts had no children at that time, but they had a lot of preconceived ideas on how children should behave. I pleaded with them to let me move some of their shiny treasures out of reach. They insisted that a child could learn to look and not touch. In twenty-four hours Debbie proved herself an under-achiever in that department. Nothing was shattered except my nerves, but they tinkled and crackled ominously. Our hosts also thought that once a child was tucked into a strange big bed instead of her own crib, she would stay there. Both Debbie and four-year-old Patty roamed the upstairs, made about seventeen forays down the stairs to check on our previous condition of servitude and finally found their way to the Land of Nod at midnight, only to fall out of bed with ominous thumps at regular intervals until dawn. I didn't notice too many tears when Anne and Micky waved us off in the morning; my eyelids were so heavy I could hardly distinguish light from dark.

I can't imagine why it took us the whole next day to travel from Hudson, New York, to Brandon, Vermont. Maybe we drove in circles. Certainly everyone inside the car except George whirled like a dervish. If I sat in the front seat with George, I spent most of the time kneeling on the seat and reaching into the back to pry apart Patty and Debbie. I know now that they didn't invent the pattern, but no matter how peacefully they might play together outdoors or in the house, after five minutes in the car each felt that the other had the preferred window, the biggest part of the blanket, or had viciously placed a small foot on the other's sacred territory. We stopped as often as a dog on his neighborhood patrol and sometimes for the same reasons. But toward dusk we pulled up in front of the Brandon Inn where we had reservations, and stumbled into the lobby. George was dragging the suitcases. I was dragging Debbie. Debbie was dragging her sniffy blanket and Patty was dragging one foot because, "It has ginger ale in it."

The desk clerk greeted us with the news that our room was at one end of the hotel on the second floor, and our daughters' room was on the other end of the third floor. He hadn't known that our daughters were one-and-a-half and four. Tempting as the notion was, we couldn't park the two little girls at that distance. There wasn't another bed available in the entire inn because a nearby camp was having parents' visiting weekend. Nothing to do but rearrange our usual sleeping pattern and ensconce Debbie and Mama in one bedroom and George and Patty in the other. Unfortunately, one bedroom had a double bed and the other only a twin bed. George took a dim view of being moiled over all night by Patty. He hauled the mattress onto the floor for Patty and slept on the springs. The double bed in my room was high off the floor. After Debbie fell out the first time, I decided to fold up the blankets and make her a little pallet on the floor next to the bed.

When the parents and the boys of Ho-Li-Satan Camp had sung their last war chant, I dozed off briefly. When I woke up and reached down to pat Debbie, there was no baby! I slid my feet cautiously to the floor and groped around on my hands and knees. No Debbie under the bed or anywhere around it. I didn't want to turn on the light because I knew it would wake her and we were both too exhausted to profit from that. So around the room I crept on my hands and knees, reaching under the desk, bumping into chairs, desk and wastebasket. In desperation I finally crawled into the closet and felt a warm, soft, somewhat damp bundle in the corner. If I'd had noonday prescience I would have left her where she was, but I thought I had to tuck her back in her improvised sleeping bag. I not only thought so once, I went through the whole ridiculous pantomime about five times that night. The last two times were easier because the pale light of dawn made the crawling and questing unnecessary. When haggard and disheveled George and cheerful Patty knocked on the door around seven, George groaned, "What a night!"

"What are *you* complaining about?" I muttered through clenched teeth. But before I could regale him with my nocturnal stalking he took off his shirt and turned around. Across his back was a double row of magenta-colored welts where the bed springs had left their imprint.

"I hope you slept well," the desk clerk sang out gaily as we descended the stairs.

"Oh sure," Patty chirped, bright-eyed and chatty after ten hours on a soft mattress. "Mommy was chasing around all night and Daddy is covered with lumps. They made us sleep on the floor."

He glanced nervously around the lobby, produced our bill with dispatch, patted the children's heads with sympathy and bustled us towards the door.

"Well, come again," he mouthed automatically, "and be sure to bring the children."

Don't Call the Plumber

WHEN WE BOUGHT the farm in Jericho twenty years ago, its plumbing facilities consisted of a creaky hand pump above the well in the back hall and an outhouse adjoining the woodshed on the indoor route to the barn. Most farmhouses built in the 1820's were similarly equipped and our great-grandmothers counted among their blessings the fact that they could make the necessary journeys without braving the elements. Of course they had to brave sub-zero temperatures, but a dry floor was a big improvement over slogging through snow from November through March, and mud until May. Fresh from the towers of Gotham we had grown accustomed to faucets and flush-toilets so that indoor plumbing ranked high on our list of do-it-yourself improvements. Do it himself would be more accurate because my knowledge of plumbing is entirely preventive. I just try not to stop up drains and toilets. My skill in re-seating the rubber thing in the back of the toilet to keep it from running the well dry was developed only after we lived in the country.

George convinced himself and me that he must be as bright as the average plumber, and that with the help of some government pamphlets he could figure out what he needed, order all the supplies in advance and put in the plumbing over the Memorial Day weekend. He and I had come up from New York two weekends earlier to plant the garden and dig the hole for the septic tank. So all he had to do in two days was install an electric pump, toilet, sink and washbasin, and string them all up like beads on a chain of copper pipes. Our proposed kitchen had been a bedroom and the bathroom-to-be was what is known in New England as a clothes press, so they were innocent of any pipes or even holes in the walls. We had appropriated a bathroom basin from my parents' attic, but the kitchen sink, the toilet and all the faucets, drain pipes, T's, unions, plugs, caps, washers, lead pipe, soil pipe, traps, threaders, pipe cutter, wrenches, blowtorch, solder, soldering paste and other items too numerous to mention were to be delivered the day he arrived.

George and five-year-old Patty drove up on Thursday. Two-year-old Debbie and I came the next day with Ken Schmidt, George's dentist friend, who was to be the plumber's helper. Neither he nor George had plumbed before. It wasn't a required course in either Cornell Medical College or Harvard Dental School. But they were friends from undergraduate days, and Schmitty supplied precision and perfection to match George's raw courage in undertaking the job.

I'm glad I wasn't there the evening George and Patty welcomed the truck from Lanou's plumbing company in Burlington. Its contents were unloaded all over the front lawn so that George could check them off his list: Gargantuan black septic tank, modest white toilet, sink, miles of gleaming copper pipe and brown bags and boxes of vital accessories. George was so absorbed in this plumber's paradise that he forgot about Patty until she came catapulting down the driveway shouting, "Look out for the cow, Daddy," and skittered past him into the shelter of the house. Sure enough, a large fawn-colored bovine was trotting along behind her, and George was about to comment to the truck driver that one of the reasons we were coming to the country was to acquaint our children with rural flora and fauna when the truck driver leapt smartly up into the back of the truck, pointed at the creature in alarm and said, "Jeesum crowbars, mister, you gotta be *careful* around them Jersey bulls." Bull? George and what now had suddenly enlarged into a very belligerent bull regarded each other solemnly over the upended toilet in mutual astonishment for a long moment, then the bull, apparently more unnerved by the

11

hardware than by George's immobility, sighed deeply and trotted off down the road.

By the time Schmitty, Debbie and I arrived, George was so eager to get started that Debbie and I were largely ignored and Schmitty was whisked off to change into jeans and a plumbing frame of mind.

For two days George and Schmitty pored over pencilled diagrams, lit and extinguished blowtorches, cut pipes and ate in a bemused fashion, a wrench in one hand and a sandwich in the other, while Patty watched hopefully to see if they would put ketchup on a pipe cutter.

When George shouted "hot lead!" we scattered like leaves as he dashed through the room with a little cauldron of bubbling lead to where Schmitty was joining two pipes under the sink. They were deaf to invitations to go swimming and dumb in any language except plumbese.

Finally on Memorial Day morning they pronounced the job done. We stood in awe as the pump was flicked on, the tank filled with pleasant gurglings and splashings and the toilet was flushed with a flourish. George and Schmitty hugged each other in a demented victory dance and toasted their skill with cold drinks.

"Look, water!" they babbled, turning on first the kitchen and then the bathroom faucets with the wild abandon of men who had crawled for days across the desert.

Then it was time for them to start on the long ride back to New York. They changed into their city clothes, and the little girls and I stood on the denuded front lawn waving them off. For the first time I was to stay in the country to face the bulls and the bats, the thunderstorms and the porcupines, all by myself. I was supposed to be grateful for the plumbing. After all, as George has pointed out for twenty years, what other woman has a sink installed at just the height she chose herself?

It all worked beautifully for several weeks. Then Patty, playing on the side lawn, called out, "Mommy, there's a little fountain out here."

I had just flushed the toilet. I tried it again and peered out the window. Up shot another geyser! I was learning to be a gardener, a paper hanger and a reluctant cowherd, but the principles of plumbing have never come easily to me. I phoned George.

I reached him at his office at the corner of 68th Street and Madison Avenue. I wonder what the patient sitting across that beautiful desk thought when George said, "Don't use the toilet. Go outdoors and whatever you do, don't call a plumber."

George fixed the geyser the next weekend. It involved taking up the lid of the septic tank and sawing off the pipe that stuck out too far into it. He doesn't recommend that job for a hot July afternoon but we didn't call a plumber. In fact, in twenty years we never did until this past summer, when in the interest of speed, not lack of plumbing skill, George had to have a new water tank installed. What's more we have had less trouble with the plumbing in that house than in any other house we've ever lived in. Never underestimate the plumbing prowess of a doctor and a dentist. I wonder if a plumber could suggest something besides, "Take an aspirin" if I consulted him about a throbbing tooth or an escalating temperature?

The Walls of Jericho

IGNORANCE may not be bliss, but it certainly leads you into jobs which in retrospect seem to have been impossible. If I had known thirty-four years ago what I know now about paper hanging, I wouldn't have had the gall to start on a 150-year-old dining room with six unmatching doors, three cock-eyed windows and pock-marked old plaster. But then I wouldn't have learned from that room and the six others that I have papered since what I know now: I am a terrible paper hanger. I'm glad I was young once, but I escape a lot of headaches by not being young any more.

We bought the house in Jericho one summer and returned for the winter to Manhattan where I browsed through the wallpaper shops on Madison Avenue until a paper with red barns and apple trees reached out and claimed me. The next summer, armed with a wall-papering kit from Macy's, my rolls of paper, and not the least notion of what I was doing, I set about papering that room.

I assumed all strips of the same length should match up side by side. Wrong. I also assumed that wall papering was unskilled labor. Wrong again. I also thought I could use the floor to cut and paste the strips. Three strikes and it was almost the ball game. I matched and hung the first two strips, but the pattern wasn't supposed to match: it alternated. The paper included three different arrangements of red barns, farmhouses, and apple trees. Put the one with the swing next to the one with the swing and the edges of the paper didn't jibe. By now my second strip was too dry to

14

remove. I had to waste a length of paper by putting another in the right alternation over it. I quietly hoped I had allowed enough extra paper for this sort of thing in my total amount. Besides, it wouldn't happen again.

I was on my hands and knees on the floor smearing paste over an eight-foot length of the third strip, when two-year-old Debbie burst through the door at the far end of my finger painting.

"Watch out for the paper!" I shouted, but Debbie was not one to brake quickly. Her tiny red sneakers grazed the gluey surface momentarily and reached for the sky as she slid smoothly on her back to the far side of the room, crashing into the wall, mouth open to wail at this sudden trick of equilibrium. The paper was unharmed. It had tracks of corduroy-wale width with hairlines down the center, but it was untorn and I smoothed it in place before attacking Debbie's gooky hair and clothes. On second thought it seemed funny to both of us, and a great improvement over the cow flop she had skidded in the day before.

A third of the job was done and I was squatting proudly in the middle of the room, trying to rub an itching spot over my eye without putting too much paste in it, when there was a knock on the door. It was Clara and Martin Powell, neighbors in their seventies, who regarded my relationship to the farm as a twentieth-century Marie Antoinette playing house in the Petit Trianon.

"Child, child, what are you doing wall papering? Not on the *floor!* Martin you go right back and get our board. We have a wonderful board for pasting paper. And I'll just look at the paste. Well, yes, it *is* lumpy, but never mind."

By the time she had smoothed my concoction to cream sauce, Martin was back with the board and had pasted a strip for me.

"Now you fold it this way," he said, deftly and mysteriously flipping it back and forth so that it looked like the ribbon candy we used to have at Christmas when I was a child.

"No, no, Martin," Clara clucked. "Not so loosely. Press it down a bit to soak the paste in."

While they argued I could visualize the paper sticking to itself and another one of my precious lengths wasted. But apparently there is no need to rush the strips from pasting table to wall, tripping over brushes, paste bucket and scissors. The longer you wait, within reason, the better it goes on. They couldn't agree on the method of smoothing it to the wall. I had a dry brush for the purpose, but only one. Martin wanted to wield that from the top down. Clara was in favor of smoothing gently with the hands from the center out to each side. Half an hour later I was in favor of going swimming. After all, the room was a third done; it was a good day's work. (Even now, on a quiet evening, I will get up and secretly compare the Powells' strips with mine. There may be some fine points of superiority in their technique but I can't detect them. Maybe the lighting is poor).

It became increasingly clear that this should be evening work, after the children were in bed. Since her jet-propelled slide, Debbie had regarded the whole job with distaste. Patty, at five, classed wall papering with other jobs that keep adults from doing important things like reading to children or taking them swimming.

Each evening I set myself the task of a few more strips. It was odd that I had not worried about the five doors and three windows. When I bought the paper they had seemed an advantage. Now it meant cutting strips down the middle and matching a six-inch strip above the door to the strips on either side of the door. The room was strewn with bits of paper, never the right place in the pattern. The whole floor was deep in shreds of newspaper and wallpaper with the annoying habit of sticking to your feet. The evenings were cool and with the stove on, the top half of the room was excessively hot, the floor damp, cool and smelling of paste. While I stood on a high-chair trying to patch an area above a door, my face was flushed, my head ached and felt light, and I descended unsteadily to the floor. In a moment my head was clear, my feet and hands uncomfortably chilly. I wished that the room could be papered with horizontal strips with the top one saved for a stoveless evening.

At last with a cavalier flourish of the brush, the room was done. Of course the strip over the kitchen and bathroom doors was made up of unmatching scraps, but maybe no one would notice. Why would our guests, sipping their coffee in the dining room, ever stare at two inches of space over the bathroom door? I don't know; but they did, and do.

Well, a job done. Gather up the newspapers, stuck to each other

and to the floor, wash out the rapidly-drying paste brush, and return the board to the Powells. It was a wide, very heavy plank and getting it into the car proved a bit of a problem. After various maneuvers involving hitting my head, pinching my arm between car and plank, and screaming at the children not to try to get in the car and on the plank while I was wrestling with it, one end settled on the backrest of the back seat and at least four feet of it stuck out the right front window. The kittens were removed; the children reluctantly moved into the front seat where they had to double up under the board. Half a chocolate cake rested squarely in the middle of the back seat where it was least likely to be sat on. I wanted to show the Powells that I could return Vermont kindness. We had been the happy recipients of Clara's famous doughnuts, and I would not return the board without a small tribute.

But the road hadn't been scraped recently and the underside of the plank was rough and coated with loose sawdust. I don't remember unloading the plank at the Powell's. I could only stare in fascination at the cake as I dumbly handed it to Clara. I dimly heard her exclaim, "Now aren't you the sly one, making a chocolate cake with an unusual topping to outsmart us country folks."

It was unusual all right. It was sawdust, shaken loose from the underside of their wide pine papering plank.

Easter Means
Another Chance

ONE SPRING MORNING when our older daughter was about four years old, she squatted beside the flower bed, poking away the sodden, dead leaves and sniffing at the moist earth.

"Mommy," she shouted, "Those old brown tulip bulbs are going to try again!"

Not all natural phenomena are accepted so simply. As a child it always puzzled me when some grownup tried to tell me that energy didn't disappear but was changed into another form. To me, the birch logs burned up, or down, into almost nothing, though I was told they were turned into heat. As a child I thought the sunlight shone, was warm and then was gone. It was hard to understand that sunlight became leaves and growth and new life.

On Easter morning it is easy to believe in life and hope. New buds, new leaves, new clothes, eggs, baby chicks. ducklings and rabbits are all symbolic of the continuity of life. Fragile, mortal man yearns to believe in immortality, whether he pictures it as a spiritual life after death, the passing on of genes, or the simple conversion of energy. I am neither theologian nor scientist but at some time most of us have been awakened to what Steinbeck called, "the terrible beauty that death gives life," whether it has been physical death or the near loss of love. The violent objection of men of good will to the experimental use of the atomic bomb is the realization that it is possible for not one country, one civil-

19

ization or one culture, but all biological life to be exterminated by misguided man. We can almost accept death as the inevitable conclusion to old age and illness. We have become conditioned to a form of acceptance of death caused by a bullet in war, but we recoil from death from a bullet in civilian life. Somehow, the tragic deaths of John Kennedy, Martin Luther King Jr. and Robert Kennedy gave their lives more dignity and beauty.

Two thousand years ago, the story tells us, the stone in front of a sepulcher near Galilee was rolled away, and Christ, the symbol of love and eternal life, walked again. Sometimes in our fumbling human relationships the stone, which has been rolled in front of love, seems too heavy to move, or the winter too long and cold to allow us to hope for spring. But Robert Frost, in his late eighties, said,

> "I see for nature no defeat
> In one tree's overthrow
> Or for myself in my retreat
> For yet another blow."

You notice he is not retreating *from* another blow, but stepping back to catch his breath and his balance *for* another blow.

Another shared moment, another crack at life, another chance to help direct our frenetic culture into more constructive channels; another affirmation that love, even though buried in the cold during a long winter of discontent, can crack through the hard earth and grow again.

The meaning of Easter to me is that no matter how huge the stone, it can be rolled aside. The stone will not disappear. It will still be there as it was beside the sepulcher, and the vestments of death will be clearly visible. But they will no longer block the passage of life and love that were lying dormant and deathlike within. Everything may not be glad again, as Pollyanna pretended, nor will anything ever be exactly the same. Why should it be? You can't go back home again, but is that what you really want? Home is not a place but a climate of serenity.

Perhaps we have to accept death before we can accept life. If death is inevitable, surely life until death is not only inevitable but ineluctable. You can't escape life until you are dead. It is not very satisfying to hide behind a stone, and preoccupation with a wound only makes it hurt more.

Each Easter we hear the story of Christ's last days. The story is familiar. We know that he is going to die. It is neither a mystery nor a tragedy. It is a love story. His death was only a period at the end of a sentence; a pause which put a frame around his life and gave it depth and perspective.

As long as we live there will always be another chance, the surge of hope that has tormented and motivated and comforted man since he began to suspect that life was love.

Pumpkins

I DON'T KNOW anything that gives a bigger return on your initial investment than a fifteen-cent packet of pumpkin seeds. A little flat package contains perhaps two dozen seeds weighing only a fraction of an ounce. Tuck them in the ground and you have a quarter of an acre or a whole backyard full of pumpkin vines that can be counted on to produce a half-ton of pumpkins, not only your backyard but probably your neighbor's, whether he shares your enthusiasm for pumpkins or not. Of course there are only a few people in the world who want a backyard full of pumpkins and I'm not one of them.

It is apparently impossible for me to plant part of a packet of seeds. If a pinch of lettuce or parsley seed is good, the whole package must be better. And who has the self-control to plant one hill of summer squash or pumpkins? A sensible gardener, that's who. We frequently have had a hedge of parsley, rows of bolting lettuce, and pumpkin tendrils strangling the beets, shading the green beans into anemia and trailing off into the meadow fifty feet from where the innocuous-looking seed was planted.

When we no longer lived on a farm in Vermont and had to adjust our rural habits to suburban Boston, we excluded pumpkins from our small vegetable garden. That shouldn't have been much of a hardship. Our girls haven't gone out trick or treating in years and theoretically they have outgrown carving Jack-O-Lanterns. Ours isn't a very theoretical family however, because both of them admitted they bought little pumpkins to have at college. Bought a pumpkin? Why, I remember when I hauled thirty golden globes down to Mark Bolton's I.G.A. store in South Burlington after we had given away the biggest and best to every child in the neighborhood. There is no such thing as having the right number of pumpkins. You either have a truck-load or none.

It all started the first summer in Jericho when we still spent the winters in New York City. I bought our seeds in Bloomingdale's, thinking that it might be nice to have a few pumpkins for pie. The packet was marked *Connecticut Field*. That was my first mistake. The picture on the packet showed a nice round, absolutely perfect, orange pumpkin with nothing to show its size in relation to anything else. By mid-July our pumpkins were the size of softballs. By mid-August they were basketball size, and by the end of August, Wayne Nealy, from whom we had bought the farm, suggested that I take them to the fair.

Ridiculous! This was the first garden we had ever planted and I hadn't known enough to plant pie pumpkins. But even if I was being teased again for being a city slicker, the best way to turn the joke was to call his bluff.

George was in New York, so the small girls and I huffed and puffed and lugged the three biggest pumpkins up from the garden. That is, I lugged and they huffed and puffed sympathetically because they couldn't lift one of the big pumpkins off the ground. They weighed nearly forty pounds apiece, and you can't carry a pumpkin that big by its stem, unless you like having your fingers perforated by the prickles or watching the stem snap off and the pumpkin crash to the ground and split. You just hug its slippery sides and stumble along unable to see over the top.

We washed our three specimens, set them on the floor of the car—no time to wash the children, set them on the seat of the car and took off for Essex Junction and the Champlain Valley Fairgrounds. As exhibitors we were given a free pass and drove through the gate to the fruit and vegetable building. The clock struck twelve and our pumpkins seemed to be changing, not into golden coaches but into much smaller, much greener, much more lopsided insignificant globes. I wanted to forget the whole thing and retreat, but how do you explain that to wide-eyed, pig-tailed little girls? So I entered our ugly old cucurbits, received the number 1356, and was told they would be judged the next day. Two days later I peeked in the newspaper for the announcement of prizes, but the vegetable awards were not published. There was a beautiful picture of the largest pumpkin which didn't look familiar at all. Now I had to know. I heaved the children into the car again, heaved the kittens out again and heigh-ho, off to the fair again, this time to pay our admission and stroll casually through the exhibits. Casually, that is, until I sidled into the fruit and vegetable building. I could see a blue ribbon attached to three enormous beauties just inside the door. But who had won the second and third places? Swallowing my pride, I asked the girl at the desk what numbers had won the other pumpkin awards.

"The children want to know, heh—heh."

The children looked surprised and I grinned foolishly.

"The second award for field pumpkins. Let's see. That's number 1356."

"1356! That's us! We won an award." Fifty cents in cash and a foot inside the Pearly Gates.

"Burlington, Vermont calling New York City. Eighty-five cents for the first three minutes, please."

"George? What do you think happened? No, the kids are fine. No, there nothing wrong with your plumbing. George, *listen* to me! The most marvelous thing happened. Our pumpkins won second place at the Champlain Valley Fair!"

O Death,
Where Is Thy Sting?

NONE OF OUR cats had nine lives, which is probably just as well. Even though our feline ranks were decimated from time to time by the calculated risks of cars, mysterious illnesses and dogs, we often had more cats than people in the family.

I must say our kittens did seem unusually hardy during Debbie's third summer. She professed great love for them and wore one tucked into the elastic waistband of her shorts as often as the kittens would permit this indignity, but her smothering attention was not always to the cat's taste. She loved to stuff them into the metal mailbox, mounted on a post in front of the house, because their tiny faces and the mailman's larger one were so wide-eyed when he opened the box. When a ladder was left leaning against the roof, she scrambled up onto the porch roof with the kittens and then quite casually tossed them off into space. They made about three somersaults en route and landed paws first, as is a cat's wont, on the grass, apparently undamaged by their venture as flying cats.

They made no effort to avoid Debbie, even though a few days later she carefully flattened them to the ground with a plank, small pansy-faces peeking out one side, spike tails and hind legs twitching out the other, and then plopped herself smack down on the board. When I leapt to their rescue screeching, "Debbie! *why* did you sit on your kittens?" she calmly replied,

"We-el, they're the only bodies around here that I'm bigger than."

A reason perhaps, but hardly an adequate excuse from the kittens' point of view.

After that summer she never subjected kittens to anything worse than being dressed in dolls' clothes or hidden under a man's hat. I must say I enjoy the latter. There is nothing funnier than a hat gliding across the floor as though by levitation, and then to see a surprised kitten emerge from under it and mince off, shaking a hind leg in disdain.

Even with the normal amount of tender loving care, occasionally one of our cats would be run over. I used to dread these accidents and the effect they might have on the children. I needn't have.

One day one of the kittens was hit by a car and killed instantly. A little later Patty and Debbie came home from playing at the neighbors and I told them, expecting tears, recriminations, or both.

"Where is it?" Patty wanted to know.

"At the corner of the barn. I'll bury it in a minute."

"No!" They both shouted in horror. "We want it. We haven't had a funeral this whole summer."

A frenzy of activity followed. Closets were dismantled in the search for the right size box. Fragrant wild roses, phlox and waxy little buttercups had to be picked, and a hole dug. Patty was seven and a half and Debbie was only five, not much use as a grave digger. In fact Patty had to jump on the spade with both sneakered feet to make a dent in the sod up under the apple trees. Debbie couldn't write either, so she was in charge of lining the box with Kleenex and flowers while Patty printed HERE LIES BLACKBERRY AGE 6 WEEKS on the inside of a cereal box top. She made another sign, too, and tacked it on a fence post: THE FUNERIL BEGINS AT THREE.

It was a lovely ceremony. The old apple tree shaded the little grave, and a soft breeze rippled across the tall grass. The little box, tied with pink ribbon, was lowered into the ground and shoved a bit to fit into the shallow grave. Both girls solemnly patted the earth in a smooth mound and covered it with rapidly wilting flowers. The marker was propped at the head after anxious whispered consultation about which was the head. Then Debbie came into her own. She was the proud possessor of a cap pistol, but she was scared of the noise. With great dignity Patty stepped up behind Debbie, put her fingers in Debbie's ears, while Debbie screwed up her face, pointed the cap pistol heavenward and fired a last salute. The deceased's siblings pounced in and out of a nearby currant bush. Mitty, the mother cat, rubbed against the girls' bare legs and murmured "Mreaow?"

We scooped up the kittens and Mitty and scrambled back down the embankment and across the road.

In a burst of emotion Patty hugged Debbie, knocking her giggling, to the ground.

"Wasn't that *fun*, Debbie? Dontcha wish we had a funeral every day?"

Lares and Penates

SHOW ME the person who has never treasured a sniffy blanket, confided in an imaginary friend, or carried an amulet, and I'll show you a deviant like me. Far from being neurotic or even tense, anxious and nervous, my friends and relations who have been or are attached to anything from a moldy hunting cap to a jade Buddha are relaxed and secure in their knowledge that help is within reach of their finger tips.

We have a doctor friend in his forties who always brings his soft baby pillow on his annual summer visit to us in Jericho. He is one of the most casual guests I know. He doesn't care whether he sleeps on the floor, in a bed or in a sleeping bag down by the brook, as long as he can tuck his little pillow under his head at night.

Ernest Hemingway hunted, fished and side-stepped bulls from Kenya to Pamplona, but never without a rabbit's foot or a smooth horse chestnut in his pocket.

I have always been surrounded by people who were tranquilized by the presence of these objects. Unfortunately, they are equally panicked by their loss. My faith in the goodness of man has been frequently strengthened by the rallying round of total strangers when one of these security symbols has been temporarily mislaid.

One such kindness was demonstrated during our first summer in Vermont shortly after we had spent a bizarre night at the

Brandon Inn trying to keep our very small children in very large beds. In our hasty get away, four-year-old Patty's "pockapeek," a small waterproof-lined cosmetic bag, had been left behind; a tragedy discovered when we were beyond the point of no return, and loudly lamented by Patty for the rest of the trip. I was reluctant to reopen negotiations with the Brandon Inn because I felt reasonably sure that their memory of our nocturnal wanderings was no more rosy than ours. But within a few days an unsolicited note came from the manager saying they had found Patty's bag, recognized its value, and would hold it until they heard from us. We were so astonished that we decided to return to New York via Brandon and pick it up.

I could have understood their concern if it had contained a wallet, keys, or even a compact, none of which was standard equipment for Patty in those days. But the little zippered "pockapeek" contained some tiny wooden doll dishes, a Fuller brushman's sample bottle of perfume and a very small, rather yellow, first tooth.

Debbie was addicted to a sniffy blanket long before Linus convinced everyone but Lucy and their grandmother that a pet blanket was an accepted household deity. As soon as she could crawl, whenever Debbie felt that the adult world had dealt with her harshly, she skibbled to her room, scaled the side of her crib, removed all of her clothes and buried her small self and her large sorrow under her pale blue baby blanket. As time and many washings went on, the blanket lost most of its nap and all of its pigment. It was as gossamer as a cobweb and about the same color. Also it was reduced in size to two limp rags each about a foot long. They looked to the rest of the world like something for cleaning guns, lining a cat's basket, or throwing into a trash can. To Debbie, Sniffy was the one constant in her changing world.

One night we arrived late and bedraggled in Fairlee, Vermont. We were too short of cash and chic to apply to the Lake Morey Club, and several motels on Route 5 were filled. But just as we were leaving town to try farther north, we saw a row of white tourist cabins and with joy claimed one of them as ours. I must say in fairness to that motel that in the intervening years both it and we have sharpened our appearance. It is very clean and gay-looking now. It was clean then, but that was about all you could say for it. The tiny living room was furnished with a high-domed horsehair settee and a wobbly little table, neither card nor coffee, adorned with a soup can filled with sand and one artificial geranium. The shower labored and brought forth a trickle of brown lukewarm water; the beds had no blankets whatsoever. Folded at the foot of each bed was a hooked rug the size of a bath mat. We were too exhausted to quibble, so we spread our coats over the beds and shivered ourselves to sleep.

In the middle of the night the beds suddenly began to shake. A brilliant light streaked through the room and the bare light bulb hanging from the ceiling danced like a cardboard Hallowe'en skeleton. Both little girls exploded awake with squawks of terror and flung themselves on top of us. There was a great roaring crescendo of noise and then the long mournful whistle of a train that apparently was about to cut our little cabin in half. We knew perfectly well that Route 5 ran close to the Connecticut river, but in our eagerness to find lodgings we hadn't stopped to think that between Route 5 and the river there was barely room for the railroad tracks. About two o'clock the vibrations started again, but our reaction was less hysterical. At six-thirty the next train served as a very effective alarm clock, and we decided to abandon the pursuit of sleep and be on our way.

Debbie was the first in the car and the most cheerful for about an hour until she suddenly wailed, "My Sniffy's gone. I forgot it in that shaky bed." She was inconsolable in spite of my monotonous recording, "You have another piece at home."

"But that was my *best* piece. It had all the smell in it."

To quiet her and keep the top of George's head in place, I promised I would write to the motel lady and ask her to look for it, fearing all the while that anyone finding that pale rag would pick it up gingerly and head for the nearest wastebasket. I wrote, however. A week later a limp little package wrapped in a brown paper bag arrived in our mailbox.

Debbie tore it open, swaddled her arm in Sniffy, and folded up on the lawn, with lowered eyelids, blissfully sucking her thumb.

You might think that she would have been cured of the habit of shedding her treasures at each port of call. You might think it, but you'd be wrong. She didn't outgrow it until she began to

31

buy her own lares and penates. One fall, when we had been year-round Vermonters for only a short while, the girls and I decided to go along with George on a trip to Bennington Hospital. Old Bennington is a historian's happy hunting ground, so while he transacted his business we went up to see the monument, the beautiful wedding-cake church and the site of the Catamount Tavern. (Little did we dream that the man who had built and lived in our house in South Burlington and who had left us the as yet undiscovered legacy of his letters in our attic was the grandson of Captain Stephen Fay, the landlord of the Catamount Tavern; and that our John Fay's parents and brothers were buried in the quiet little cemetery we walked through that afternoon.) We were only tourists then, but eager ones. Nouveaux Vermonters are prone to be.

When we returned to the hospital, George was ready. There was just time for a dash to the ladies' room before starting back to South Burlington. Debbie thought it advisable to take her doll, Arithmetic, as well. No, I don't know why she was called Arithmetic. As a matter of fact Debbie can't tell me now except that to a first grader the name had a grownup ring. It was a matter of sound rather than symbol. In any case we whisked in and out of the ladies' room with a minimum of time spent experimenting with soap dispensers, hand dryers and vending machines.

Somewhere south of Rutland Debbie's banshee wail lifted us off our pre-safety-belted seats.

"I left Arithmetic in their basement."

Once again guess who volunteered to write and ask if Arithmetic, a doll, had been found in the ladies' room of the Bennington Hospital.

There is an advantage in having a package mailed from a hospital. They have all sorts of authoritative labels on hand to aid and abet the swift progress of serums and anti-toxins. A box marked "Rush," "Medical Supplies," "Immediate Delivery" was delivered by special messenger to George's office in the medical school. His secretary was nonplussed when she opened the official looking package and saw Arithmetic's battered face smiling up at her. The entire family voted to send a box of candy to the volunteer ladies who had wrapped her carefully and mailed her with dispatch to shorten a little girl's time of mourning. Debbie snatched Arithmetic out of the box with the mixture of joy and anger familiar to every parent at the moment of regaining a lost child. She scolded. "I can get along without you when I know you are here, but I can't get along without you when I know you're *not* here!"

The Pig's in the Meadow, the Cow's in the Corn

YES, I KNOW it should be sheep, but during our years in Vermont it was more likely to be pigs.

We didn't have a little boy blue. We had two little girls pink, instead, and they didn't waste much of their valuable blowing time on horns. They went through phases of blowing bubble gum which exploded and stuck to their faces, and they had plastic balloons that gradually wrinkled and drooped in rubbery wads on the kitchen counter. But, no horns. There was a bugle—reserved for a special use. When guests were expected at our farm in Jericho, it was traditional for the girls to climb part way up the hill to a vantage point near the big pine tree, and blast off when they saw the right car coming. This got them out from under my feet in the kitchen during the last hour, moaning: *"when are they going to come? Huh, Mommy? When?"* It also gave me about three minutes' warning so I could put on lipstick and remove a wet bathing suit from the one upholstered chair in the house.

But, back to the cows in the corn. In our nine winters on one farm and eighteen summers on another, we never kept cows. This was because the farmer's wife (me) was too lazy to milk twice a day and pasteurize the milk, only to be told later that "it tastes funny." We were surrounded by dairy farmers though; and guess who spent as much time as possible on our land? Everybody else's cows.

You would think that a cow in the middle of a nice grassy meadow would stay there and eat the nearest clover available. That is what you'd think but you'd be wrong. Placid and unplotting as she looks, a cow will find the one weak spot in a barbed-wire fence and stumble through it, catching her hind hoof on the sagging wire and pulling down another fence post.

When I looked out our kitchen window and saw a cow grazing under our apple trees, I would enjoy the pastoral scene for one thick-headed moment. Then the return to reality, which is to say, "Oh-my-gosh, the garden!" The cow, with extrasensory perception, would have the same thought and with Pavlovian response was already salivating and heading for the corn. Before she had time to decapitate more than a few stalks, I was bearing down behind her, hurling epithets, sun-baked clods of earth and a few, small, ever available rocks. Off she would gallop the full length of the garden—never in one path between the rows, but crossing it diagonally, trampling tomato plants, beans and broccoli as she fled. How could I complain to our neighbor, when he, his brother and his sister and brother-in-law had been out straight, the day before, helping me corral our wandering young pigs?

Our pigpen was very secure and pig-proof—for big pigs. It was a former horse stall, with solid wooden walls on three sides. George had boarded the front opening with three or four planks at about three-inch intervals. How two six-week-old piglets, who measured at least seven inches in diameter across the midriff, could get through a three-inch space, I don't know. Perhaps over the top? One morning I went to feed them and instead of snorts and scuttlings under the shavings, there was an empty pen, an ominous silence. I heard little snuffling sounds at the back of the barn. Before I could reach the snufflers, they had scrabbled past me out the door and into the wide open spaces.

Stupid as I was about many aspects of farming, I had no illusions about my chances of catching two small, fat pigs careening around a six-acre field—unfenced. They have to be cornered, lunged at, missed and after at least twenty tries, finally tackled. It is hard enough catching them in an enclosed pen, but at least

there you can grab a leg and hang on while your ear bones vibrate with their protests. Lacking these circumstances, I ran back to the house, and phoned our neighbor, Janice Hill. She alerted her brothers and I went out to get the bearings on the piglets while waiting for the alerted brothers. The two pigs meanwhile were rooting and snuffling happily in the meadow. The hay was short enough so that I could see their rounded rumps darting here and there, out of reach. When Ed and Pud, the Hill brothers, came trotting cross lots, we reconnoitered and circled. From three sides of the field, trying to close in on our quarry, we stalked them. We drew our noose very quietly, but, as Pud lunged, missed and sprawled flat, the other piglet ran straight into my outstretched arms—and out again. We ran. They ran. We circled. They circled, always together, wheeling and swooping as though guided by some invisible radar. The day was cold. Puffs of steam from the breath of three human beings pushing forty, and two piglets pushing six weeks, exploded in little dyspneic spurts. We closed in again, whereat they wheeled and scuttled towards our driveway. They clattered up the graveled driveway. We sprinted after them. They dashed across the highway, practically under the wheels of a huge construction truck, skittering into Rollin Tilley's driveway just as Rollin and Helen came out their kitchen door to aid and abet. My fingers were numb with cold. My body was dripping wet and my pulse was pounding loudly in my ears. As the pigs and Ed and Pud and I thundered into their dooryard, Rollin threw a huge net over our elusive porkers. We—me—everybody hurled ourselves on top—of the net, the pigs, and each other. I was gasping for breath, from exertion and also because a large, booted leg pinned me to the ground. Ed was sitting on Pud's head. The rest of Pud twitched and struggled to get free by kicking Helen in the face with a rubber-soled work boot. Tears rolled down Rollin's red face and the two little pigs squirmed and squealed miserably under the net. I was too exhausted to get up and collapsed, panting, until Rollin and Pud each worked a pig out of the net and grasped them firmly by the hind legs.

We made a triumph out of the return to our barn. When the piglets were once more snuffling in their shavings, Rollin nailed the front opening *solid*. He used three-inch nails and all the strength of his two-hundred-pound frame. The sound of his hammer rang out like the Anvil Chorus in the day's frosty air.

Rollin regarded his handiwork from all angles. "Shouldn't wonder if they'd take the rest of their meals right about here," he commented.

A Place for Everything

A PLACE for everything and everything in its place is one of my husband's unfulfilled dreams. I'm for it too with things like my pen, the car keys and Go-Go records, though the spot I'd choose for the latter would be at a considerable distance, well out of ear shot.

During the years when George was Dean of the Medical College at the University of Vermont we ran a Noah's Ark, ferrying our furred and feathered friends from our winter home in South Burlington to our summer home in Jericho and back again each September. We found that the term "barnyard animals" was euphemistic. Slowly and imperceptibly, in the way that cellar holes of abandoned farms fill in with wild raspberries and fire-weed, our barnyard animals began spending more and more time in the house, while I seemed to spend more and more time in the barns.

"I can't wash the dishes; the ducks are in the sink," is probably the most unusual excuse I heard during the period when our two daughters subscribed to the belief that any work in lieu of play would make dullards of them both. I must admit I preferred a sinkful of ducklings to a sink full of dirty dishes. They would waddle across the drainboard like fat old women, plop heavily into the water and sail off serenely, their golden fluff floating lightly on the surface. Then with a flick of their tails, they would dive straight down to inspect the drain.

I have absolutely no resistance to baby wild rabbits, ducklings

38

and wide-eyed, steeple-tailed kittens. I can stop after the second handful of semi-sweet chocolate bits and the fifth, no, the sixth ripe olive, but those Easter card babies turn me into a blithering idiot.

Of course, most of the time the animals were outdoors or in the barns, sheds or chicken houses. The horse never set hoof over our threshold. The pigs did not darken our door until they had been metamorphosed into hams and pork loins. But Michael, the goat, was a frequent and funny visitor, skidding stiff-legged across the rubber tiles of the kitchen floor and usually ushered out unceremoniously within a few minutes because of his habit of dropping "raisins" when under emotional stress.

"Lambie," a full grown ewe, stupid, vacant-eyed, dirty and otherwise typically sheepish, spent two weeks in the cellar with her lamb, Jackie Gleason, because we were twitchy about Jackie's chances of survival in the cold barn. In retrospect the cold barn might have been less traumatic than being, in the house, a sheep among Wolfs. Jackie was hauled up the worn old cellar stairs every afternoon to be hugged and squealed over by Debbie and her third grade classmates. Perhaps little girls with new teeth too big for their faces, knees too knobbly for their matchstick legs, and Brownie uniforms too wide through the shoulders and long in the hem, felt a special affinity for this woolly lamb whose skin, hooves, voice and knees were equally ungainly.

As spring advanced and the sheep returned to their fold, a converted horse stall, you might suppose us to have cleaned out the hay bedding circled by snow fence that comprised their home away from home in our cellar, restoring the basement to the spiders and an occasional mouse. You might suppose it, if you didn't remember that nature abhors a vacuum, and during our prolonged attack of animal husbandry, so did we.

No sooner had the cellar lost some of its sheep aroma than we installed twelve-day-old turkey poults in a big homemade cage that looked like a four-poster bed enclosed in chicken wire. The wire mesh floor of it was two feet off the cellar floor, to keep their big clumsy feet warm and dry. They had a heat lamp overhead, glowing day and night, which, each spring, sent our electricity bill sky-rocketing. They had a waterer which smelled like disinfectant because that's what was in it. They also had special starter-mash and small grit, both of which they walked in until we taught them how to eat by lifting their feet out of the feeder and shoving their beaks into it.

Why all this bother when we had a perfectly good henhouse fifty feet from the kitchen door? Because there were two dozen laying hens in one side of the henhouse, one hundred chicks under a brooder in the other side, and everyone had told us that we must *never* mix turkeys and chickens. You can't even walk from a henhouse into a turkey house without carrying the droppings on your shoes and infecting the turkeys with black leg, or is it black head? Anyway we had been so thoroughly brainwashed into thinking it was the Black Plague that never the twain did meet during the first six weeks of the turkeys' lives.

When we moved them up to Jericho each summer the turkeys graduated into an outdoor, raised, covered pen and the hens went into the barn and woodshed. By then they probably could have mingled without dire results. One year when we brought the turkeys back to South Burlington we let them run loose around the yard from September to Thanksgiving. By then they were five months old and weighed from ten to fifteen pounds. They were too stupid to realize that they could have wandered across the fields and into the woods and swapped the certainty of the ax for the uncertainty of eluding the foxes. They strutted across the lawn and driveway, giving the homestead a Currier and Ives appearance.

Maybe we were too cautious. I only know we never lost a turkey from black leg when they were started out at separate tables. Of course a neighbor's dog got two that year, a weasel or other rodent killed another once in the Jericho pen, and one turkey committed suicide by hurling himself against the side of the pen and breaking his fool neck. It doesn't take much to panic turkeys, and when they rush hysterically to the nearest corner they may trample each other to death if the pile-up gets too deep.

There were drawbacks of course in harboring the young poults in the cellar. One was that I had to remove the newspapers spread underneath the cage every day and dump the droppings on the asparagus bed. Even so, when you opened the cellar door in the kitchen, the turkey smell was overpowering. They also fluttered and flapped and kicked up quite a cloud of grain-dust and feathers which sifted down on the washing machine, the rows of home-canned vegetables and pickles and the hair of anyone foolhardy enough to spend much time in the cellar. But it was worth a few sneezes to watch the faces of uninitiated guests in the living room directly above the turkeys. Many of our guests were fresh from the towers of Gotham. If they arrived in May they were spellbound by the fields aglow with dandelions, the apple trees unfolding in bloom, the first lilacs smelling like Mary Chess perfume, and an oriole gargling liquid silver in the elm tree. Mesmerized by all this bucolic bounty they collapsed on our couch and stared into the depths of a drink-on-the-rocks or glass of wine. Stupid and un-predictable as turkey poults are, ninety-nine percent of the time their sense of timing at this witching hour was perfect. They were silent the first half hour. But when the ties and tongues of our guests had been slightly relaxed, up from the depths of our one-hundred-and-fifty-year-old cellar came a flurry and flutter; an exact replica of what is called a ruffle of drums. As the visitors warily eyed each other and their glasses, the overture began.

"Wheet-wheet-wheet," and then all twelve big poult beaks wid-ened in a whistling chorus, high pitched and piercing.

"What is *that?*"

"What?" I would ask naively.

"That whistling. It sounds like it is right underneath us."

"Oh, *that*. It's just the turkeys in the cellar."

It was worth the smell, the dust and the long hours of plucking that still lay between me and Thanksgiving dinner.

At least we were the ones who put the sheep or the turkeys in the cellar and the ducks in the sink. The cats had more leeway in their choice of habitat. Theoretically they lived in the barn, but from time to time we were tolerated by a house cat of such dignity and wisdom that he or she was the major-domo and we were suffered as slaves. Mr. Cat preferred to sleep out, but spent his days looking like an ornamental black panther stretched full-length on our scarlet sofa. He was benevolent and undemanding and made his few wants known by an almost inaudible "Mra?" Mitty was content to be a barn cat when she wasn't pregnant, which wasn't often. But as soon as she gathered girth she espoused family

life wholeheartedly, human and feline. If we sat in the living room, so did she. When the girls went up to bed, she was up the stairs two leaps ahead of them and purring loudly on one of their beds. Small wonder that one night Patty called downstairs, "There are funny noises in my doll carriage. I think Mitty's had her kittens in it."

Sure enough, the doll carriage, appropriately furnished with small pillows and blankets, swayed under the shifting weight of one large black cat and five blind, wet, groping kittens. And Mitty's unblinking gaze, glowing green from the reflected hall light, made her position clear.

A place for everything, and what better place for newborn kittens on a cold night than in a doll-sized baby carriage?

Who's Afraid
of the Big Bad Sow?

WHEN WE LIVED on the farm in Vermont, it was a shock to discover that on the rare occasions when we needed a vet, his house call (or should I say barn call?) cost more than my husband had charged his human patients for a much more thorough going-over in his office at 68th Street and Madison Avenue. But it wasn't the price that unnerved me. It was the very active doctor's helper role that I had to assume when we were unwilling to let unwell enough alone.

The time I have in mind didn't even involve a sick animal. It involved twelve, very healthy, baby pigs and their overstuffed mama. They weren't all patients, but they all got in on the act. So did I. For a while the only not-so-innocent bystander was the vet.

We had raised pigs for years, buying a young barrow and a young sow each fall and spring, and raising them until they reached the best-edible size of about two hundred and twenty-five pounds each. But one year we decided to keep the female and have her bred, thinking that the price we would get for her offspring would offset the cost of her feed over the winter. It didn't, of course, but we couldn't have bought the fun and education that litter provided.

When we reclaimed our sow from her visit to a nearby farm,

the farmer had told us the expected date of her accouchement, and George wrote it down on the calendar. A pregnant pig looks so much like any other full-grown pig that we frequently wondered if she was in the family way. As the date approached, she didn't give any evidence of impending domesticity. She didn't paw around and try to make a nest the way our ewe did on similar occasions. Her eating habits were the same wholehearted dedication to food that she had exhibited from infancy, and I wasn't quite enough of a hog midwife to examine her for dilation even if she had let me. But on the night of the proposed date of her confinement, George's curiosity got the better of him, and he set out for the barn with a flashlight just to show that he hadn't forgotten.

In three minutes he was back in the house, wide-eyed, open-mouthed and breathless.

"Come on," he gasped. "Come and look. There are thousands of them. I couldn't count. The whole pen is swarming with tiny oinkers."

We dashed back to the barn as we were; I in bedroom slippers, Patty and Debbie in pajamas. Debbie was foaming at the mouth with toothpaste, toothbrush still damply clutched in her small fist. George hadn't exaggerated. Mama looked just the same, grunting and snuffling, surrounded by twelve, rotund, miniature copies of her own blimpish figure. There were copper-colored ones, red and white ones, black and pink ones, calico ones, and one or two pink piglets. We counted and recounted, always coming up with a different number—twelve, eleven, thirteen. We couldn't believe it and the girls could hardly wait till morning to tell the occupants of the yellow school bus about our population explosion.

The babies were named and renamed for presidents, baby sitters, TV heroes and athletes. We often climbed into the pen and grabbed one out to play with. Mama would just grunt softly and tolerate our unwonted foolishness.

Then one day our neighbor commented, "You'll want to get the young boars altered before they get much bigger." Altered? I knew that when we had bought six-week-old piglets the male had always been de-tusked and castrated, but it had been a *fait ac-*

compli and I had never given much thought to how or when.

Well, certainly it was nothing George had learned in medical school and besides, the thought gave him gelatinous knees. Having killed the only young rooster I ever tried to caponize, I didn't volunteer.

I called the vet. To my surprise he seemed willing and able, and only asked that someone be there to help him when he came the next day.

I was there all right, but he glanced uneasily over my shoulder and asked if there wasn't a man around. There wasn't. George was at the office and I didn't want to tell the vet that my doctor husband had felt queasy at the thought. He shrugged his shoulders and proceeded to the barn.

"You got the sow in with them?" he gasped. "She'll tear us apart if we touch those young ones."

"Oh, no," I reassured him. "She's as gentle as a lamb. We get in the pen and pick them up all the time. She only gets excited if a stranger gets in."

"Well *I'm* a stranger. I'd rather chum up with a wild boar than a sow with a litter. If you say so I'll give it a try. I'll grab a boar and hand it to you and then you hang onto its hind legs no matter what."

He climbed into the pen. Mrs. Pig snuffled around his boots and began to make low rumblings that vibrated the whole length of her 400-pound frame. He reached out to grab a small hind leg, and she charged. At least I think she charged. All I know is that the vet catapulted over the side of the pen spinning me sideways, caught his foot on the top board and sprawled on the barn floor.

"I guess you were right," I murmured weakly, hoping he wasn't going to sue us for abrasions and contusions. "Maybe I can lure her into the horse stall and shut the door to that side of the barn."

Fortunately mama pig accepted my offer of a pail of mash and followed it meekly into a box-stall. I hastily bolted the stall door, shut the door to that part of the barn, slid the bolt, and returned to the babies.

From there on everything went like clockwork; that is, if you are used to clocks that squeal like twelve small pigs being murdered, plus a mother clock whose muffled roars of disapproval made the beams quiver. The funny thing was that the little females who weren't even touched shrieked as loudly as the little males who were being cut quite unceremoniously without benefit of anesthesia. They not only squealed, they dove, scuttled and scrabbled until caught; then they thrashed and squirmed while I manfully struggled to hold each one by the hind legs and ladyfully looked the other way. As luck would have it, we had more males than females, and though the vet was quick, skillful and hardly drew blood, he and I were covered with sweat and less attractive substances produced by the frantic young pigs. As soon as each pig was castrated, the vet set him down and he trotted off without a peep of pain or regret over the loss of his boarhood. When they were all done, we let mama out just before she demolished the horse stall. She made a bee-line for the babies, sniffed them over with obvious distaste for the antiseptic smell, and promptly lay down to suckle her brood.

The vet sat down and held his head in his hands. His shoulders heaved convulsively, and I glanced away in embarrassment, not sure whether he was weeping or having a seizure. Finally he threw back his head and snorted aloud with laughter. In relief and exhaustion I leaned against the pig pen and whinnied. He mopped his damp red face with an oversized handkerchief and wiped away the obvious tears that were streaming down his cheeks.

"If you could see your way clear," he choked out, "not to advertise the way I flew out of that pen, just for a while, till I get established in my practice here, I'd certainly be beholden to you."

He's very well established now. I've never seen him since, but this summer we drove past his place and I saw that he has enlarged his house, built on a whole new animal hospital and hardtopped the driveway. I'm sure it's all right now to advertise. I waited quite a while—ten years.

The Apples of My Eye

THAT OLD SNAKE in the garden of Eden was an amateur. If he had been a professional troublemaker, he wouldn't have stopped after urging Eve to take the first bite. He would have suggested that she and Adam make cider out of the remaining fruit.

It was not pure chance that an apple was the golden fruit of discord that led to the fall of Troy. From the Garden of Eden to the market place in Switzerland where William Tell had a nervous moment, apple fanciers have bobbed, curtsied and fought for this fruit of their labors.

Greek and Roman mythology, folklore and early American history are as stuffed with apples as a deep-dish pie. And although Johnny Appleseed chose a more southerly route west with the seeds he gathered from the cider mills of Pennsylvania, he had kindred spirits in Vermont. When the first settlers moved up from Massachusetts and Connecticut to claim land in the Green Mountain state, apple trees were often planted before the fields had been cleared for corn.

It is impossible to think of Vermont in spring without immediately seeing an old apple tree in bloom, or in the fall without baskets of McIntoshes and Northern Spies circling the still heavily-laden trees.

It was no surprise, therefore, when we inherited apple trees with the old farmhouse we bought in northern Vermont. Only six trees, two Macs, two Spies and two Baldwins. At first they were more beautiful in May than bountiful in September, but George pruned them in March, sprayed them at the required and always inconvenient times through the Spring, and we were both delightfully surprised when the branches bent to the ground with sound, fragrant fruit in the fall.

> "And pluck till time and times are done
> The silver apples of the moon
> The golden apples of the sun."

went round and round in my head as I clung to the wheel of the red truck and lurched across the frost-slick meadow to our little orchard, awarding myself the pleasure of leisurely apple picking as soon as George and the girls were off to office and school.

There is nothing more crystalline than a late September morning in Vermont after the sun has burned off the first white streamers of mist. Aching arms are scarcely noticeable when the Indian-summer warmth wraps around your shoulders. A twig in the eye is unimportant when, with your good eye blinking, you can look up through leaves to patches of unbelievably-blue sky. Even when your sneakered feet are pinched to numbness in the narrow crotches of the branches, the discomfort can hardly intrude on senses surfeited with the fragrance of bruised windfalls and ripening leaves, the contrast of crisp breeze and warm sunlight, rough bark and satin-smooth apple skin.

But after picking the first few bushels with tender-loving-care for several idyllic mornings and then urging, cajoling, and finally bribing the children into perforating their skins on the twigs, it seemed that for every apple picked, two reappeared overnight.

We ate them raw, peeled, sliced; dropped the slices in salted water and froze them; made applesauce to eat and to freeze; made pies and baked them; made more pies and froze them; gave away bags of apples; urged our neighbors to come and pick them; fed the windfalls to the pigs and to our omnivorous chickens.

"Still climbing trees in the Hesperides?" quipped a scholarly neighbor, noticing my simian gait as I swung through the aisles of the supermarket.

At breakfast every morning we would watch a doe and two yearlings stepping daintily through the meadow grass under the

apple trees. They seemed phantom creatures in the autumn mist until, with the help of field glasses, we could see the flick of their white flags and the plumes of their breath strung out on the frosty air. We didn't begrudge the deer their share of the windfalls. I would gladly have stored apples to feed them all winter, but we knew that with the first day of the hunting season we would see the deer no more. The cautious doe would hide them deep in the thickets of blackberry and hemlock until the footfalls of the hunters were no longer heard in our woods.

We ran out of methods of using the apples long before we ran out of apples. So we dreamed up visions of cider for Hallowe'en, cider and doughnuts after school, cider as gifts, cider for Thanksgiving, and vinegar for next year's pickles.

Now that we were drunk with our visionary brew, we became ruthless about picking. The children happily shook the branches and who cared if the apples were impaled on the sharp stubble beneath the trees? We tossed the sound fruit, the misshapen fruit and the deer-nipped fruit into the back of the truck. We shook out our empty feed bags and stuffed them full of apples. We begged and borrowed empty jugs from the sheds and attics of our neighbors and scrubbed out the dust and folded-up spiders.

With about a quarter of a ton of apples, twenty gallon-jugs, two adults and two children in the truck, we set off for a cider press near Camel's Hump recommended by the man at the lumber yard. We later discovered an excellent cider mill much nearer, but in the early years we seemed to have a knack for choosing the path of most resistance.

The Huntington area is wild and lovely. You can leave the highway at Richmond and in two miles become lost in woods where bear and bobcats still surprise the deer hunters.

After a variety of wrong turns, encounters with deaf residents, dumb resident and vocal dogs, we finally catapulted into the dooryard of the cider mill, unloaded our apples and watched the owner begin to dump our apples, now well-coated with dust from our feed bags, into the top of the press, adjust the cloths, turn the screws and after a great rattling and thumping, a pale golden stream began to trickle out of the spout into our motley array of jugs.

No money changed hands. The owner of the press took his fee in cider. We loaded our jugs onto the back of the truck, swathed them in the empty grain sacks to keep them from bumping each other and breaking, and returned home in triumph. Everyone had a glass of cider. Delicious! Everyone had another glass and we admired our display of amber jugs. The third day no one seemed quite so enthusiastic about cider. The girls reverted to milk and peanut butter sandwiches after school. By the fourth day I noticed there was a new zing in the taste of the cider. The girls said it had turned into ginger ale and surreptitiously tilted their

glasses into the sink. George pretended to like it, but I drank it with more loyalty than love. Along with the fizz it had also developed an oddly sour taste. Probably the dust from the grain bags was adding its complex complement of the ingredients of chicken mash and pig feed. By the end of the week it really tasted awful. We didn't dare give it away. Oh well, it would still make splendid vinegar. The ridiculousness of nineteen gallons of vinegar for a family of four was too obvious to dwell upon.

So we lugged the nineteen gallons down the hundred-and-fifty-year-old cellar steps in five and a half trips each, set them in a cool place near the bushel baskets of apples and the row of golden pumpkins and forgot them in the pressure of other harvest chores.

Several weeks later, George was in the living room one evening conducting a meeting of a medical college advisory committee from all over the State, when there was a retort like a gunshot in the cellar. I pressed my ear to the cellar door and listened. Pop! and a long hiss like escaping steam. I opened the cellar door warily, and a smell reminiscent of the open cellar doors on Bleecker Street, when the Italian families were making wine, billowed out through the house. Fsst! went another, and in rapid succession the corks from the other sixteen jugs ricocheted off the old, adzed beams of the cellar. The ceiling, the floor, the apples, the pumpkins and half the cellar were bathed in our pale amber strong-smelling, sour mash brew.

To the eternal glory of the distinguished committee members, Vermonters all, no comments were made, no questions asked, no nostrils twitched. If we chose to run a still or swab down our cellar with hard cider, it was obviously our business. The business of cleaning up the mess was obviously ours too.

It was quite a long time before a taste for cider returned to our house. It was an equally long time before the smell of cider departed from our house.

But the tart, crisp, hand-dried Macs lasted through till Christmas. The Baldwins were still hard in January. We baked the frozen pies in March and the last jar of applesauce was finished just before I started out the next September to pick the first of the next year's crop.

And now, apart from Vermont at that time of year, when the yellow school buses start on their appointed rounds, when the smell of burning leaves drifts through the hazy September air, I am haunted by the memory of our crimson Macs or the striped green and scarlet of the Northern Spies. We can never again taste the Northern Spies, for the interstate highway mowed down those two trees. The two McIntoshes and the two Baldwins still stand, but the people who now own our old house in South Burlington are separated from the little orchard by fences and two lanes of hurtling traffic. The waxed apples in plastic bags at suburban markets have taken on the flavor of wax and plastic. They are too far and too long from the tree. And I yearn again to bruise my feet in the crotch of a gnarled apple tree, to reach for the reddest apple from the highest branch within my grasp, and to lean back against the rough grey bark and taste the fruit that will always be worth the risk of exile from Eden.

A Burden of a Beast

BETWEEN the dark and the daylight, when adolescence is beginning to lower, comes a pause in a girl's preoccupation which is known as the horsy hour. Just about the time when Patty had built up an immunity to mumps, chicken-pox and prickly heat, she came down with a severe case of equinomania. It is a disease more prevalent in female children than in males. Often it is one of those sex-linked heritages, like hemophilia or premature white hair, that seems to leap from the males of one generation to the females of the next. Perhaps if my father had carried the gene for horsitis he would have passed it on to me. But as a boy growing up on a farm which he couldn't wait to leave, my father regarded a horse as a beast of burden and I, in time, came to regard it as a burden of a beast.

George didn't show his true racing colors at first. When Patty began to ruin every Saturday morning by wailing about her underprivileged, culturally deprived, horseless environment, he was sufficiently motivated by economy to point out that horses were enormously expensive. Patty was undeterred. She clipped ads of horses for sale. Her conversations were larded with "Annbabcock has a horse, Susan Deslauriers has *two* horses, Murryjane is going to get a horse, she thinks." I welcomed Susan's invitation for Patty to ride one of her horses, thinking she might find out that Pegasus was a myth and return to pop-it beads and hula hoops. Instead she came home with bruises on her derrière, stars in her eyes, and enough verbal ammunition to barrage us for several Saturday mornings to come.

After all, she argued, we already had a barn with a horse stall, about fifty acres of pasture and plenty of hay. She would earn the money for oats by selling our old newspapers to the waste paper company at a half-cent a pound.

George showed signs of weakening emotionally but not financially. I am Mrs. Noah when it comes to aggregating animals and a sucker for gratifying the whims of the young, but I nursed a guilty secret. I was horse-shy in spite of having had riding lessons as a girl. These I had promoted solely because they gave me status in high school.

Both girls assured me that I would never have to saddle the horse, pitch hay into or manure out of the stall. They were right on the first count. I still don't know a snaffle bit from a whiffletree, and I think martingales ought to sing by moonlight in enchanted forests or at least be woven out of cobwebs and worn by milk-white unicorns. My hands may have been unsullied by saddles, but during three of the best years of my life I pitched down a whole loft full of hay, pitched out a mountain of manure which was spread out over our fields to become another loft full of hay and repeat the back-breaking cycle.

Anything can happen in Vermont and in our case invariably does. I knew from Patty's first tantrum that the net weight of our livestock was about to be increased by about a thousand pounds. It just happened that Patty's sixth grade teacher's daughter had a horse and was beginning to emerge from the horse phase and look with more favor on a boy. This is the standard pattern of a girl's focus of attention: Brownies and exclusion clubs from nine to twelve, horses from twelve to fourteen, and boys happily and unhappily ever after. Maybe there is something to be said for horses after all. At least they are stabled or put out to pasture after dark, their top speed never exceeds second gear, and their upkeep, if you live in the country, costs less than cheeseburgers, pizzas, milk shakes and cokes.

Donna Harvey was willing to part with her horse, if it went to a good home where she could visit it occasionally. George was willing to adopt a horse he didn't have to pay for, and Patty had a

civil tongue in her head for the first time in months. Lady, a small mahogany-colored mare, made the seventy-five-mile trip from her summer home in Craftsbury to our winter home in South Burlington without any ill-effects. But George, struggling to maneuver a truck that swayed and listed every time Lady moved from one side to the other, was sicklied o'er with the pale cast of nausea by the time they drove into our yard.

For a while our establishment was Mecca for all our children's schoolmates. Flat-topped and Tonied heads popped up in the meadow and around the corner of the barn at all hours. Once Lady was caught and saddled she was obliging about giving rides around the fields. But she preferred the leisurely pace of life with the young stock in the pasture and went to a lot of trouble, mostly ours, to avoid being caught. She would amble up to the pasture gate readily enough when we came out for her, curling back her prehensile upper lip in anticipation of an apple, but at the sight of the bridle she would daintily step back out of reach, toss her head, clamp her yellow teeth shut, or occasionally nip Patty's shoulder.

Bridled at last, she would follow along meekly and play cowboy, landed gentry or knights of the Round Table, depending on

55

whether Debbie, George, or Patty was in the saddle. Sometimes from the kitchen window I would see both girls riding her bareback, their jeaned legs swinging limply as they rode through "South Pass" into "Camelot." I would pause in my potato paring and bask in the idyllic scene. But nothing remains idyllic very long when it involves children and animals. Our life never seems to be a series of snapshots, but a moving picture—a little too moving now and then.

One day I had driven out of our yard in the truck leaving Patty, Dudley Moor, and Tom Hart peacefully taking turns riding Lady in a wide circle in our front meadow. I wasn't away more than fifteen minutes. (Of course I couldn't have done anything if I had been home except avoid the embarrassment that I was not.) Returning from Bolton's I.G.A. store a mile away I rounded the bend in the Hinesburg road, saw a riderless horse galloping wildly down the road towards me, the saddle swinging underneath her belly, the stirrups flapping grotesquely on either side. Not just any old horse, a very familiar horse: Lady! She dashed past me, eyes rolling, sweat-darkened and terrified at the sound of the stirrups whacking the pavement. I jolted to a stop, turned the truck around in the nearest drive and took off after her, wondering where and how whoever had been on top of her was now. I could see Lady ahead, careening crazily from one side of the road to the other, but between us there was a car. I was frantic trying to think how to let the driver know my predicament. I needn't have been. He saw *her* predicament, and as I followed helplessly behind, he executed a series of quarterhorse techniques with his green sedan that turned the Hinesburg road into a snowless slalom. He drove slowly behind her, turning and twisting to keep her in the road. At the parking lot behind Perley Blanchette's garage he made a wide circle, headed her into the far corner of the lot where a fence and Mark Bolton's store made two barriers, parked his car across her exit, got out and calmly walked up to her and grasped her bridle. By the time I pulled up behind and catapulted out of the truck, both Lady and I were humbled, shaken, and grateful.

The inevitable crowd of small boys sprouted out of the gravel. Patty and our neighbor Rollin Tilley roared up in Rollin's truck.

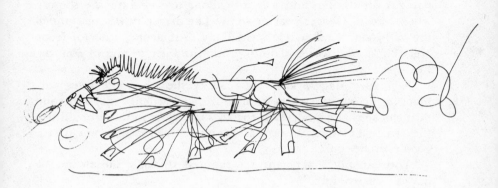

I was getting the story from an ashen Patty. No one had been hurt. One of the boys had been leaning down from the saddle trying to pick up a jacket when the saddle loosened and he fell off. When Lady took off, she caught her leg on the barbed-wire fence. Patty had run all the way to the Tilleys' barn to get Rollin, arriving so breathless and frightened she was speechless. He finally got the gist of the crisis and he and Patty had roared down Hinesburg Road in his truck.

Now Rollin was examining Lady's bleeding leg, everyone was talking, Lady and I were panting, and my knight of Hinesburg Road, the cowboy in the green sedan, disappeared, unknown, inadequately thanked, his praises unsung until now. I wonder who he was. I'll probably never find out and he will join the ever-swelling ranks of quiet Vermonters who simply reach out a hand to start a car or stop a horse, and go quietly on their way.

I drove the truck home in low gear with Patty sitting on the tail gate holding the reins loosely while Lady limped meekly along behind. We lost most of our retinue of small boys after the first half-mile. Patty and Lady were once more in good spirits, but the truck and I were somewhat overheated by the time we clattered into our gravelly drive.

I left the truck in the driveway to cool off, put Lady in her box stall, carried four pails of water out to the barn for her, climbed up in the loft and pitched down a mountain of hay. Then

I fed the pigs, fed the chickens, gathered the eggs, cut some asparagus for dinner, and was just about to step into the shower when I heard George's car drive in. The driveway was just under the bathroom window. He was talking to someone, a doctor from New York, who was exclaiming over the bucolic joys of country life.

"Say, does Maggie know how lucky she is? Apple trees and lilacs in bloom, vegetables from your own garden, eggs from your own chickens and a horse for the kids to fool around with! I'll bet they are real cowgirls by now and it must give Maggie some pretty good exercise too."

"You can say that again!" I shouted through the steam. "I haven't the strength."

Which Came First,
the Chicken or the Egg?

I HAVEN'T the least idea which originally came first and I'm not going to be lured into one of those heated and point-less arguments about it. In our case the chicken came first because we wanted eggs and we didn't have time in those early years, when we only summered in Vermont, for day-old chickens to grow the five months they require before they will ovulate for the break-fast table.

We had a barn with a horse stall that could be converted into space for about twelve laying hens. It wasn't the sort of chicken coop you'd see in a poultryman's magazine. It wasn't the sort you'd see anywhere except in our barn in Jericho, because it was dreamed up and constructed out of George's ingenuity, a small amount of chicken wire, and second-hand lumber. One end of the horse stall had a sort of drop front where there were several boxes, presumably for oats. With a little hay they made cozy nests, just the way laying hens like them—dark, enclosed, and private. Hens will lay eggs right out in the open if they can't find a hidey-hole and the urge is strong upon them, but they really seem to prefer a little dark, dry spot where they can meditate quietly before and gloat after they have given up the egg. So after George had in-stalled a false floor of chicken wire at waist height across the horse stall, and made them a dandy feeding trough, with a compartment at one end for oyster shells and little arched wires on top so they wouldn't roost on it, we were all set. The open chicken wire would allow the droppings to fall through to where they could be shoveled out by guess who? Of course it would allow a lot of grain and oyster shell to fall through also, but inasmuch as all the chicken droppings were destined for the garden, we told ourselves that the oyster shells would add calcium. We didn't discuss the spilled grain.

We set off for a neighboring farm where there were laying hens for sale and in the cool and dark of the evening (so they would be sleepy and somewhat tranquilized) we moved twelve plump, softly-muttering hens into a crate and then into their new house.

The next morning we could hardly wait to go out and peek into the nests. Eureka! Two large, rose-beige eggs in one nest and a hen on the other. I gingerly slid my hand under her and was rewarded with two more eggs and a sharp peck on my wrist.

Nothing equals the beauty of a new-laid egg, warm, smooth with delicate almost translucent coloring. It is a living color, like skin. Patty and Debbie fought for the privilege of carrying in the eggs, and one promptly squashed in two-year-old Debbie's starfish hand, although she "hardly fweezed it." For several days it was almost impossible to keep four small hands out of the nests. For the next two summers and the following nine years when we lived year-round in Vermont, it was almost impossible to get them to darken the chicken-house door.

A dozen hens provide a small family with a plethora of eggs, more than four dozen a week. Luckily there wasn't much cholesterol talk at that time, and we enjoyed the abundance and the lowered meat bills. There are only two things wrong with fresh eggs. They are much harder to de-shell when hard-boiled than their elders in the super market, and they consistently refuse to stand tall on the top of a lemon meringue pie.

When we bought the house in South Burlington and inherited a real, if aged henhouse, we decided to spread out a bit. George divided the henhouse into two compartments. On one side were our old girls, the laying hens; on the other side, a hundred day-old chicks in May, who turned into broilers in August if they were boys, and into laying hens in October if they were girls.

With the Agricultural College of the University of Vermont only two miles away, I felt I should take a course in poultry raising. There must have been about a hundred boys in the class. I was not only the only woman in the class, I was exactly twice the age of most of the students. But what I lacked in youth I made up in enthusiasm. After all, I had a working laboratory at home and an economic reason for taking the course. I got the second-highest mark in the class on the final exam and humiliated my children by boasting about it. Fortunately it was a written exam, and the physiology of the hen bears a remarkable resemblance to the physiology of the frog I had dissected in Zoology at Mt. Holyoke. On the practical side my record was less distinguished. I was such a crusader that when we learned to caponize the young males, I not only removed the little lima-bean-like testicles, I cut an artery as well and killed my young rooster!

Theoretically I also learned to cull out the hens that were poor layers. It sounds easy enough. You look around for pale dry combs and pale legs; then you pick up the pallid one by a quick swipe at her legs, tuck her under your arm upside down and examine the vent which twitches convulsively like a mouth trying to stop a sneeze. If the vent is dry and puckery and the space between her pelvic bones won't allow four fingers to lie flat between them, off with her head! The only trouble was that often when one of my rejects was opened up, she'd be stuffed with eggs in various stages of maturity from little golden globules to full-sized, extra-large, complete with shell. I didn't do too much boasting about my "cullinary" ability. But inasmuch as I was the only one in the family who knew anything about culling, or enjoyed up-ending our feathered friends, my laurels didn't require much looking to.

That course had an exotic fringe benefit, a small brown South American hen named Arky. Mr. Donald Henderson, the head of the poultry department at U.V.M., was doing research in crossing breeds. He had imported some wild fowl called Araucanas that are believed to be the forbears of our barnyard biddies. When they hatched some of the Araucana eggs at the experimental poultry farm, he offered me a small female. When she was tiny, our other chicks, like young human beings, seemed to have no racial prejudice, and treated her as though she had come from some place with chicken status like Rhode Island or Plymouth Rock. But as soon as they lost their down and feathered out into lanky adolescents, she became a target for fowl play. They made her eat at the second shift at meal times. They shoved her off the roost until she learned that her place was at the end of the roost, nearest the cold window. Her wild genes stood her in good stead, however. She lived with us for four years and turned out pullet-sized, blue-green eggs so regularly that the others should have been jealous. Maybe they were. At any rate she was worth her light weight in the bewilderment she caused among our egg customers.

It was our habit to sell our excess eggs to a few of my husband's colleagues at the medical school and two or three neighbors whose children referred to me as "the egg woman." Our eggs were so fresh that I took pride in dating them, even to the day of the week, so that our customers could use them in the order of their appearance. When Arky joined the production line, I thought it would be funny to slip one of her blue eggs into the Monday spot each week. I expected instant repercussions. No one commented on the appearance of one small, blue-Monday egg among eleven beige two-and-a-half to three-ounce eggs. I repeated the performance. No reaction. I finally realized that the silence was indicative of the Vermonter's reluctance to having his leg pulled, especially by someone from "away." At last, Brad Soule, head of the X-ray department and a friend and egg customer of several years' standing, phoned in defeat.

"All right," he said. "I give up. I've spent hours in the library. I've looked it up in ornithological books. I've even asked the rabbi, who has identified it as a wild bird's egg. *What* is it?"

It was two weeks before our Jericho friend and neighbor, Wayne Nealy, admitted that he had tried to wash the blue off, had candled it, shown it in strictest confidence and secrecy to a few cronies, and finally had opened it cautiously, out on the back porch at night when the family had gone to bed. Too bad that shy little Arky never knew that as another lady from "away" she had given me those moments to offset the many times I had had to join in the laughter at my ignorance of established Vermont customs.

Almost every aspect of our new farm life taught us something far more important than a new skill in dealing with an unfamiliar task. The first summer, when our imminent return to the city of New York made it necessary for us to dress off our laying hens and freeze them for future consumption, we approached the task with mixed emotions. Of course we had planned to eat the chickens, and we hadn't really developed any emotional attachment to them as pets which could spoil our appetites. But neither of us had ever killed or plucked a chicken, and I had only watched them being eviscerated at the butcher store. Besides, we weren't sure what effect this mass murder would have on our two-and-a-half and five-year-old daughters and decided they would be better off visiting their friends down the road. The children were apprehensive and reluctant to be parked. I was equally apprehensive but impatient to get on with the job, so I shoved them inside Clara Manor's door and raced home.

Back at home, I lugged the old copper boiler out onto the manure ramp behind the barn. Then I heated water and lugged it to the boiler. George in the meantime had sharpened the ax, caught a squawking hen and appeared, weighted down with both and an expression as lugubrious as a professional mourner's. While I held the hen's feet and looked away, he lopped off the head and I flung the hen far out on the grass where it leaped and twitched convulsively, making strange noises through a windpipe that no longer led to its beak. As soon as it was still I snatched it up and dunked it in the hot water; then we both squatted down and started plucking. I think it took us half an hour to pluck that first hen. The wet feathers stuck to our hands, our jeans and our noses when we tried to brush away the large iridescent flies that were attracted to the scene. A hen couldn't have that many feathers. The first hen hadn't been dunked long enough, and each feather put up a good fight. I dipped the second one too long, cooking the skin slightly, so that it tore in patches. By the time we had done six it was noon, most of the feathers had been transferred from the hens to us, and we were confirmed vegetarians.

When I brought home the children, they surveyed the scene wide-eyed and silent; then they stared at us in the same horrified way. There was no doubt that even at a mile's distance they had been through a traumatic experience. It suddenly dawned on us that it was our apprehension and not the butchering that was frightening. George suggested that they help when we dressed off the other six chickens. To my enlightenment as an ex-nursery school teacher and armchair psychologist, it turned into a gay affair. They loved watching the headless chickens flop! They and their pet kittens raced out to pick them up and plunge them into the hot water. They fell to and plucked fistfuls of soggy feathers with delight, and were fascinated with opening up the hens, turning the gizzards inside out to see what the hens had been eating, finding eggs in various stages of development, and cutting open a liver and a heart to see what they looked like inside.

On the sunny, blood-and-feather-strewn manure ramp, with kittens mewing, flies buzzing, and children up to their elbows in the warm depths of a chicken's abdomen, I learned that what they had feared was not blood, entrails or dead chickens. They had been scared of the unknown and the atmosphere of anxiety. We shield our children from birth and death, from frustration and danger, and then we wonder why they find it so difficult later to accept frustration, danger and life. Never underestimate the power of a dozen dumb biddies to knock a little sense into their human counterparts.

Do Ladies Drive Trucks?

"My face, I don't mind it
Because I'm behind it
The people in front get the jar."

This was brought home to me a week after a red, half-ton Ford pickup truck became our second car. Of course I had been initiated gradually. When a second car became a necessity in our family, I had been entranced with the Army Jeep we bought, even though children had a tendency to fall out the back, and icy winds had more than a tendency to whistle in around the canvas and ising-glass and nudge me in the front seat. We needed something useful and rugged to fit my role as a country wife. My husband, as Dean of the Medical College at the University of Vermont, could only farm as much as his wife's back could stand. The Jeep had limitations in space and comfort, so after remarking kiddingly to each other, "What we need is a half-ton truck," we finally realized that a truck *was* what we needed.

George drove it home victoriously one afternoon, and the next day I steered it happily along the main street of Burlington and parked in front of Preston's jewelry store with as much pride as though it had been a Mercedes Benz. As I was about to leap to the ground, a small boy tugged at his mother's coat and gasped,

"Look, Mommy, a lady in a red truck! Ladies don't drive trucks."

He wasn't criticizing my character. He was stating a fact based on observation. He would have been equally surprised to see a lady on a fire engine. For that matter, so would I. Of course I never saw myself driving the truck. I thought George looked pretty funny, driving it in a black Homburg, a relic of his Madison Avenue practice days. And Patty looked as though the truck were driving her, when she perched behind the wheel. I was so happy inside the truck that I never gave my image a thought. It was the handiest conveyance that ever shared our garage with a "soft car." You had a panoramic view high in the cab surrounded by wide windows and no chrome gadgets. It held twelve Brownie Scouts with the sound of their songs and squeals mercifully streaming out in our wake. Several bicycles could be slid easily into the back; any number of skis, grain bags, ten-foot planks, and even our horse, whose name inappropriately perhaps, was Lady. Without the truck we couldn't have moved our menagerie of pigs, sheep, kittens, turkeys, children and other assorted lares and penates from South Burlington to Jericho and back each summer. We would have had to change our habits, and habits are harder to change than conveyances. It was useful to our friends as well. Ethan Sims used it to move old beams that had been part of the spire of the Unitarian church. John Teal borrowed it to transport a horse either to or from his farm on Camel's Hump and he was used to transporting musk ox calves by plane from the arctic tundra to the sub-arctic climate of Huntington.

It was a wonderfully versatile vehicle, with none of the short-comings of a "soft car." Melted popsicles, shavings and pig manure could be washed out in a few minutes leaving nothing clinging, either literally or by a not too subtle hint of fragrance. When we went *en famille* to Maine in the "soft car," Debbie's starfish that she had carefully collected from the tide pools left a fishy aroma in the trunk that we had to live with until we turned in the car. A scratch or dent was a major catastrophe, but the nicks and gouges on the truck were only battle scars that enhanced its character. The chassis was so high off the ground that we could hurtle up lumber roads or across the fields without being hung up on a boulder or damaging all those useful things like exhaust pipes and axles which they tuck underneath. The mechanism under the hood seemed simpler and much more accessible to me. If it didn't start on a dewy morning, I could identify the spark plugs, wipe them off with Kleenex and be on my way. If it conked out after a long haul over dusty and sandy roads, Patty taught me that a sharp tap with a hammer on that big round thing in the engine loosened the grain of sand and off we roared again. There was no trunk to lock your keys into by mistake and no cloth upholstery to capture and preserve the prints of little feet.

Of course it was a bit trying for our teen-age daughters to be picked up in front of the high school by a mother in a red truck. But when you are thirteen and fifteen anything your mother does is unbearable. They would scrunch down as far out of sight as possible and plead with me to make a fast get away. But the truck gave them a certain rapport with the high school boys who were thumbing rides up Main Street, and often we had collected three or four healthy specimens before we had climbed the hill to the U.V.M. campus. Given the choice, the boys would have preferred a sports car or any car without a muffler which would have called attention to themselves, but when the choice was between Shank's mare or riding in the back of the truck, where they could war-whoop or whistle at passers-by, depending on the sex, they leapt over the sides, spraying books, track shoes and large feet with no damage to the truck. I can think of a dozen young men now in Cambridge, Oklahoma, the Virgin Islands or the Navy with whom I had frequent, limited and identical conversations, "Thanksfer-theride" and " 'Sokay."

As a matter of fact our truck wasn't really conducive to conver-sation. The driver couldn't hear what the boys in back would have, thank goodness; and it was probably just as well that they couldn't hear an occasional blasphemy from the front seat.

In fact one time the truck was a real conversation stopper. We had been invited to drive up to Greensboro, a distance of sixty-five miles, for luncheon with old New York friends, Beth and Roudy Roudebush. It was an annual pilgrimage which we en-joyed. A few days before this I had been overambitious in loading crates of chickens into the truck and the muscles of my back wouldn't let me forget it. Driving a car was the most painful posi-tion. Sitting in it was almost as bad. In fact the only pain-free position was flat on my back. So George inflated a rubber mattress, put it in the back of the truck, gave me a pillow and a blanket and we set off for our rendezvous in total, if isolated, comfort.

To shield my eyes from the sun I pulled the blanket over my head. I could see through the blanket but no one could see my face, a very entertaining arrangement. I watched the clouds, pi-geon-blue underneath, white cotton candy on top; jet planes pre-ceding their sound by half a sky, an oriole slipping down into her pouch nest slung from a high branch of an elm, bright-blue, top-halves of silos and square, rosy brick chimneys. George came to a stop in a village and I found myself directly under a large maple that harbored two unusual birds. They were telephone repair men, booted and spurred, and presumably cutting some branches that interfered with the wires. At least they were until our truck pulled up underneath them. One man stared at my inert form decently covered except for a protruding pair of shoes, nudged his helper who exclaimed, "Good Lord! It's a body! Just layin' there, no coffin."

"What you think he's up to? Taking it across the border?"

That was too much for me. As George started up again, I slowly raised my hand, in my best imitation of a corpse and waved what I hoped looked like a sad farewell to this life.

I've always been sorry George didn't see their faces. Far from showing relief, they were open-mouthed, pop-eyed, and stricken dumb.

A moment to savor, and it never could have happened without our old red truck.

School Buses

I HATE TO ADMIT that I have never been inside of
a yellow school bus. Not that I've hankered to do so, but it labels
my youth as part of what our children call "the olden days." My
lack of familiarity with the inside of a school bus doesn't mean
that I was conveyed to and from school in a surrey with a fringe
on top. I walked, scuffing my brown Coward shoes through piles
of crimson and orange leaves in the fall, squeaking on the hard-
packed snow in my arctics, stylishly left open so that their black
metal fasteners could flap, or stepping gingerly around the naked
and hopefully limp worms that littered the slate sidewalks in the
spring.

In my childhood the yellow school bus was not an intermittent
part of the landscape or a constant drain on the school budgets.
Perhaps that's why I have no nostalgic feelings about these saffron
leviathans that lumber singly up the dirt roads through the Vermont hills, or nose to tail in a great river of ochre out of consoli-
dated school parking lots.

Our children had to cope with the literal and figurative pres-
sures of hours of confinement in school buses. True, I transported
them on foot or by car to nursery school and, in Patty's case, to the
Brearley School for two years, until we moved out of Manhattan.
As soon as we moved to Vermont for good, the school bus began to
delineate our day as surely as the alarm clock and the ten o'clock
news.

It used to be said that almost anybody could be governor in

Vermont, and that almost nobody usually was. This fortunately hasn't been true in recent years, but it is still sometimes true of school bus drivers. In many cases we hand over our orthodonted, vitamin-stuffed, Salk-swallowing young to the not-so-tender mercies of some character we wouldn't trust to mow the lawn, even with grandpa's hand mower. Sometimes not only do they not know the children, they don't even know their appointed rounds, and lean heavily upon the navigation of the children until at least Columbus Day. Of course there are exceptions. There are probably thousands of dedicated conscientious school bus drivers all over the country. That's the trouble. They are scattered so widely that the presence of one comes as a shock to both children and parents.

Mrs. Goodhue in Jericho knows how to turn the terrors of a first day at school into triumph for a six-year-old. And Mrs. Shepherd in South Burlington was an exceptional woman in or out of the school bus. Even on the ground she made you feel that you were a tiny sailboat being borne down upon by the *Queen Mary*. But when she mounted her golden chariot, the combination of this large imposing lady in a large yellow bus was awe-inspiring. The parents revered her and always hoped they would be on her route. The children had mixed feelings. It was comforting to know that you wouldn't be tormented by the class bully or have your lunch box raided while you rode behind Mrs. Shepherd's majestic back, but it also limited your own chances of showing off or hamming it up a bit. There was no nonsense on her bus, and nonsense included almost everything except sitting perfectly still and bolt upright, your feet dangling several inches off the floor until your own house hove into view. Mrs. Shepherd knew every child, where he lived, whether he started out with two red mittens, and whether the baseball bat under his seat belonged to him or the seatmate he had just left.

We weren't lucky enough to live on Mrs. Shepherd's route. The first time that Debbie rode the bus home from first grade, the bus didn't spew her out along with our Patty and the clutch of children who got off at our country corner. Patty skipped down the lane reveling in her freedom, unconcerned with Debbie's whereabouts.

"Wasn't she on the bus?" I asked.

"I saw her get on but everybody pushes."

"Couldn't you call to her to get off at our stop?"

"It would take half an hour for her to get up to the front of the bus."

I knew that she had either been swept off at the wrong stop by the tide or was still on the bus flattening her nose against the window anxiously looking for landmarks. I needn't have worried. Twenty minutes later there was a phone call from neighbors two miles farther down the road. Debbie was there and would I like to retrieve her? She was quite unconcerned and reported that from the time they left the schoolyard she had been trying to make her way to the front of the bus, but the big kids were so "thick" that it was just as Patty had predicted. It had taken her more than half an hour to reach the front.

By the time that she was one of the "big kids" they had a bus patrol and she was one of them, an older child who sat up front and leapt out smartly at each stop to try to monitor the exodus and cut down on the number of children squashed when the driver closed the door too quickly.

Even with this improved status the bus ride was always noisy and fatiguing. Too bad they can't walk to school as we did, unwinding all the way home; making plans, rehearsing speeches, daydreaming, gathering horse chestnuts or lobbing a few wet snowballs at each other. By the time we got home we were relaxed and ravenous, a part of the community and attuned to the seasons in a way unknown to these over-privileged children who only see life darkly through the glass windows of the yellow school bus.

Wayne Nealy, Vermonter

THE FIRST TIME I saw Wayne was the August day we stopped at his store in Jericho Center in 1948 to get a few stamps and a pair of jeans. He spotted us instantly as newcomers— summer folk and probably labeled us quite accurately as young city folk, eager and gullible. We had rented a converted barn in Underhill for August but were looking for a summer place to buy, a little farm preferably with a brook, dammable or ready-made for swimming. He stared up at the ceiling, harumphed a few times and then said, "Well, there is a place up the West Bolton road, with a nice pool that might be for sale."

Of course it turned out that he owned it. It was his birthplace, his father's farm, and had been empty and more or less on the market for ten years; less if the buyer was undesirable and familiar with its assayed value, more if someone gave promise of caring for it and wanted to pay the asking price. We did, and began a friendship of nearly twenty years that had all the give and take, the tart flavor and the sweetness of a taffy pull. I loved Wayne and he loved me, but neither of us could bring ourselves to show it except for trying to out-wit or out-racont each other until he was almost at death's door and I was two hundred miles away.

Contrary to local opinion, which was that we had paid too much for it, the purchase of the Nealy farm in Jericho was the best investment we ever made. We paid a good price but we got full value, and a bonus in friendship beyond price. Wayne and his son Ralph kept their cows on our place for the first years. They mended fence and paid the electric bill. The cows kept down our pasture and the Nealys kept the hay. Morning and night during the summers when I was there alone most of the time with the small children, the muffled clink of the milk pails in the misty dawn, and the answers to my interminable questions at afternoon chore-time gave us the better part of the deal.

Wayne would give you his shirt, but if you were to buy his shirt he'd get his original price for it. When our heating stove arrived after we had left, he and Ralph set it up for us. When we came up for the summer, Wayne's wife, Anna, sent out biscuits or doughnuts, followed by her famous white raspberries, beans and squash. Wayne taught me how to plant potatoes, where to find blackberries, how to thin paint and how to putty a window. In fact he puttied a good many of our windows. But if I paid him one cent short for the milk we bought from him, he'd call my attention to it, and we never asked for or received credit.

There was a streak of chilliness in his attitude toward us for a while after we bought the farm, and it was just by chance that I found out why. When we bought the farm we asked a Burlington lawyer to search the title. Well, sir, Wayne had been town clerk for twenty years. He knew every deed like the back of his hand and he knew every inch of that farm like the front of it. So he interpreted our legal intervention as a doubt of his integrity and it took a while for that wound to heal. Anna knew we were young and foolish and forgave us for it. Wayne knew we were young and foolish, and thought it was high time we grew up.

The fact that we served a much shorter apprenticeship than is customary before we were accepted in the village was largely because of Wayne's and Anna's sponsorship. They introduced us in the store, in church, and included us in chicken-pie suppers as though we were their son and daughter. They became a third set of grandparents to our girls. Known as somewhat cantankerous to the schoolchildren of the village, Wayne would stand patiently behind the candy counter for fifteen minutes while Debbie, her nickel clutched in her sweaty little palm, deliberated on the comparative merits of wax pipes, licorice strings or hard little brown barrels. When Debbie would wander up from the brook, clad only in her untied sneakers and twirling her bathing suit from one finger, Wayne never batted an eye. When Patty asked what artificial insemination was all about, he told her without an ounce of self-consciousness or double talk. When the little girls sneaked into the back of their car at milking time and hid, giggling, Ralph and Wayne, perfectly aware of the maneuver, drove off nonchalantly and feigned great surprise and consternation when the girls leapt up and "surprised" them a mile down the road.

When anyone stopped in at the store, which was also the post office, to ask where we lived, Wayne gave them directions and then immediately phoned us so that we would be forewarned.

"A New York car with five people, all of them large and hungry-looking, heading your way. Need anything from the store when we come up for chores?"

One summer Wayne had a fainting spell or a heart attack in Bennington and was put in the Bennington Hospital for observation. He liked to be observed about as much as a catamount and he didn't figure on tarrying there a couple, three days. His son, Robert, was driving a hearse east for delivery and at the moment had stopped to visit his mother in Jericho. So into George's custody, as a doctor, the Bennington authorities agreed to release Wayne if George, Ralph and Robert came down and drove him home in the black ambulance. The return trip was uneventful. Wayne, in a hospital Johnny coat, lay meekly in the back. But when they got back to the store, Ralph and Robert tried to carry him up the stairs to their apartment on a stretcher. They had to tilt the stretcher to get around the corner. That was too much for Wayne's dignity. He was back in his own bailiwick and he didn't aim to make an entry trussed up like a wild boar. He loosened his bonds, leapt off the stretcher and, with the tails of the short Johnny coat flapping, stamped barefoot up the stairs reviling modern science with all the fervor of a latter-day Ethan Allen. Ralph, George and Robert bit their lips and didn't dare explode with laughter until Anna in her quiet way had smoothed Wayne's ruffled feathers.

I think I worried more about Wayne's reaction to my

book, *Anything Can Happen in Vermont,* than about the reviews. He had told me the first story in it, he had lived through many of the episodes, but if he felt that any part of it showed Vermont in an unfavorable light, I would not only hear about it, I would probably be banished from the state. I needn't have worried. After I sent him a copy he wrote:

Jericho, Vermont

Birthplace of *Anything Can Happen in Vermont*

Dear Mrs. Wolf—Your VERY interesting book acknowledged and read first to last chapter all with great interest on my part; my particular interest was in "The Law and I," for nothing "buggs me" more than having to pay into those darned meters for the right to spend my money in Burlington; thank goodness we do nearly all out of town business in Essex Junction and so avoid the street parking in the city. . . . My thanks for the book which I have read and will read when I get blue and need cheering up as long as I live.

Sincerely, Wayne

I'm glad I didn't see Wayne during the last months of his life. It was a terrible indignity to him to be bed-ridden and dependent. The last summer, I stopped in one day to share with him some of the letters that had come in about our book. I told him that one man had written asking how to make sausage that would taste like the kind his grandfather used to make.

Wayne was silent, his face pale and waxy on the pillow, his eyes closed. I thought perhaps he was unable to hear me.

Then he opened his eyes and in a voice weak but crackling with his old spirit he said, "That's easy. Tell him to send you the pig his grandfather made the sausage out of."

I hope there is a heaven, because he wanted so much to be with Anna again. I rather think there is because if he had gotten to the other side and found he'd been fooled, he would have come bustling and harumphing back to set the records straight.

Diana the Huntress

HUNTING has never appealed to me. It is not only that I am solicitous for the feathered and furry folk; I am scared of the noise. I don't like cap-pistols or firecrackers or trucks that backfire in front of me going down steep grades. Being unable to keep my fingers in my ears and on the trigger at the same time, I leave the shooting to George. The smell of gunpowder makes him close his eyes and dilate his nostrils in the same dreamy, anticipatory state I experience when I smell roast beef cooking. He likes to look at guns, hold them, squint up or down the barrels and of course shoot them.

In spite of this George does not hunt, and most of his shooting is really target practice. The five cows who were upon the land when we bought it didn't belong to us, though we were on very cozy terms with them. The pigs, though ours, were not for shooting; neither were the chickens, the turkeys, the sheep, the horse or the two kittens. We know that deer browse on our land. A large buck was killed by a car in front of our house the day before we went up last June. We've seen one marten, an occasional fox, a mother raccoon and three babies playing hide-and-seek around the maples on a summer night. George shot an elderly, slow-moving porcupine one of the first summers, but was eager to bury it and forget the whole thing. He felt an unfair advantage over a prey who waddled slowly a few feet ahead of him.

Woodchucks are a recurrent nuisance. They can shear off the young string bean plants in a night. Our first summer there was a woodchuck hole in the woods on the east side of the garden and another hole, or set of holes, fifty feet south of the garden, right out in the open meadow. Our garden never showed a bit of damage that year. The hole in the woods may have been abandoned, probably the morning after the garden was ploughed. We became quite familiar with the woodchuck who lived in the meadow. Often as I walked down to the garden he would rise up on his haunches and stare at me, derisively I thought. I was a bit paranoid about my gardening that first year. I would snatch up a handful of stones, always plentiful in a Vermont garden, and throw them in his direction while he remained where he was, aware that he had nothing to fear from my aim. Then I would charge down upon him while he leisurely dropped down on all fours and made a dignified retreat into his hole. One morning I found this too insulting to bear and filled his front and back door with the mounds of dirt piled near them. Whether this discouraged him in any way I don't know. I doubt it. I think he just became bored with watching me. This performance only happened from Mondays to Fridays inclusively. Mr. Chuck never cared to watch George on the weekends, or perhaps he never cared to have George watch him.

Woodchucks don't seem to be in danger of extinction in New England. The next summer the two sets of holes near the garden appeared to be abandoned, but across the meadow where a line of trees follows the curve of the brook, a woodchuck appeared one Sunday morning.

"George," I whispered hoarsely, though the woodchuck could never have heard a shout at that distance, "There's a woodchuck. Look out the living room window."

There was a crashing scramble and window opening and a shot. The woodchuck looked interested, a little surprised, and ambled off into the trees.

Nothing would have surprised me more than if George *had* shot him. George has more confidence in his marksmanship and made off to the meadow with an empty tin can. He returned, got the range and perforated the can. Why any woodchuck would visit that scene again I can't imagine unless out of sheer curiosity, but the next morning there he was in the same spot, investigating the can. This time we all ran around to the back of the house and stood on the mound over the septic tank to watch. George had his gun, I had my fingers in my ears, Debbie clutched me around the knees, and Patty and the kittens leapt up and down in excitement.

The woodchuck must have heard us. He stood up on his hind legs, beautifully exposed. A shot—he dropped down, rolled over and started crawling slowly away. That wasn't what we'd had in mind. A dead woodchuck is one thing; a wounded one could not be ignored. We wiggled under the fence, scrambled and skidded down the steep pasture, under the next fence, galloped across the wide meadow. I was in the lead, unhampered by firearms, George next, Patty right behind; Debbie panted "wait for me," and the two black kittens leapt in little arcs in the rear. Eager to atone for my gunshyness, I crashed around through the trees, sure that Mr. Chuck was making for his hole. Sure enough, there was a brown tail slowly disappearing into it. I grasped the furry tail and dragged out the heavy, faintly struggling body. The children and kittens were beside themselves with fear and excitement, shrieking and mewing as I bore my trophy out into the sunlight. He was badly wounded. George pushed the children behind him and shot the woodchuck again quickly. The kittens, driven by some age-old instinct, leapt upon him fiercely. But the lure of the chase was over for me, and I felt only amazement and sadness that we had wanted to kill this animal. The return trip was in reverse. Kittens and children dashed proudly ahead to tell Mr. Day, the mailman, while George and I followed rather shamefacedly with the gun and the woodchuck. The hunting season for Wolfs was over.

Give a Tradition
for Christmas

WHAT SHALL WE GIVE our children for Christmas? Plastic computers? Wet suits? A round trip ticket to the moon?

The stores and mail-order catalogues are filled with an incongruous assortment of shiny luxurious gifts, "conversation pieces," treasures that will be cherished for a lifetime and baubles that will be broken or forgotten before the tree begins to shed its needles.

Each season, millions of packages will be wrapped and unwrapped, some given with love and understanding, some given from a dull sense of obligation. The gift that never ends up in the attic or in the roaring maw of the apartment incinerator is the gift of a tradition which, like old silver, becomes more beautiful with use.

A child, like a plant (or an adult) likes to put down roots. Children love to establish little patterns which give them a feeling of being a part, not only of the immediate family, but of the past and of the larger family of the world.

We are particularly fortunate in our country because we have

81

such an international heritage of Christmas traditions; the lovely crown of lighted candles and flowers worn by the girls in Sweden; the wooden shoes on the doorstep in Holland; *Bûche Noël* from France; *panettone* from Italy; Christmas carols, yule log, mistletoe and plum pudding from England, the *piñata* from Mexico.

Most of the traditions of Christmas have to do with immortality. Some of them originated long before the birth of Jesus Christ but were taken over by Christians as symbols relating to his birth and life. The Romans used to celebrate Saturnalia with green wreaths and candles, which they gave to each other and carried in processions through the streets. In the eighth century the Germans began the custom of bringing evergreen trees indoors and lighting them with candles. The door wreath originated in the United States but has spread to other countries as a sign of welcome during the holiday season.

The evergreen trees or boughs, the long-burning log, the lighted candles, and the star of Bethlehem all symbolically assure us that life, and therefore hope for mankind is eternal.

This feeling of continuity and good will, this unbroken chain of hand clasping hand from the Druids and the Romans to the stable in Bethlehem to the huge tree in Rockefeller Plaza is the gift that our children unconsciously desire, will keep for a lifetime, and pass on to their children.

The gifts of many Christmases that, even in memory, bring the wonderful warm feeling of Christmas, were the smell of the kitchen when my mother was making applesauce cakes, stirring the marmalade, and roasting the turkey; the earnest voices of the red-nosed carollers from the church singing under the front window; or the prickly but aromatic job of balancing the Christmas tree while my father struggled to adjust the wobbly stand of crossed boards.

I was particularly grateful at Christmastime when we lived in the country in Vermont, where it was possible for us to drive out to our little farm in Jericho and cut our Christmas tree on our own land. Like all of life's memorable experiences, these expeditions were half comedy, half tragedy. The day was always bitterly cold and the woods were hushed and deep with snow. When the children were little this meant red, aching fingers and loudly expressed misery when a hemlock bough unloaded its burden of snow down a small neck. There were always as many opinions about which was the right tree as there were members of the family. George's patience grew brittle and he shouted for a unanimous vote.

Finally and with many misgivings, the tree was chopped down and lifted out into the open. Invariably it looked smaller, less well-shaped, skimpier than we had thought. But woe to him who voiced such heretical opinions! It was our tree and we were proud of it. If it was turned a few inches and some branches draped at the base, no one would notice that it was practically flat at the back. We might have suggestions about improving its appearance, but even the littlest child would have been ashamed to call it ugly. It was now a part of the family, to be teased a little, helped and ornamented, but certainly never to be scorned.

On the trip back home in the steamy cab of the truck, with sniffling noses and feet of marble, we burst into Christmas carols. George turned basso profundo and embellished "The First Noel" almost past recognition. "Rudolph the Red-Nosed Reindeer" seemed strangely appropriate after the solemnity of "O Holy Night."

We have other little family customs too. We continue to hang stockings at the fireplace even though the girls now shake out lipsticks instead of dolls' bottles. We cut out cookies in star and bell shapes and decorate them with colored sprinkles, then burn half of them while we dash upstairs to shove an exposed present under the bed. We exchange homemade things with the neighbors, pickles, fruitcakes; we admire their trees. Suet puddings steam in coffee cans. The youngest child grinds the celery, onions and dried bread for the turkey stuffing with such gusto that it crunches underfoot for days. The tree is lighted after many maneuvers with snarled wires and defective bulbs. If the ground is bare, there are repeated anxious glances out of the windows until someone shouts, "It's snowing!"

Our old farmhouse creaked and braced itself against the wind. It had celebrated Christmas for a hundred and fifty-two years. The first Christmas goose was roasted in an open baker on the hearth, the last in the electric stove. But the fragrance was the same, and the wonderful hushed excitement on Christmas Eve was the same, when we finally turned out the lights and paused a moment to look out the front door, across the white fields to the tiny squares of yellow lights in our neighbors' houses.

We haven't been able to give peace on earth to our children. But we can give them the heritage of all the Christmas traditions that mean good will toward men. Perhaps they will be able to follow the star of Bethlehem with clearer purpose and more confidence.

Out of the Sap Bucket into the Bean Pot

YOU CAN'T PULL yourself up out of the cool sweet depths of a Vermont sap bucket and dive into the Boston bean pot without experiencing cultural shock. That's a term the anthropologists bandy about a good deal these days. It seems to mean that when you move from one culture to another, you're not much use to either one until your head and heart follow your feet. They used to call it homesickness.

After ten years in the north country, the old crimson tie looked, at first glance, a little like a garotte. They tell me it is worn a little more loosely than formerly, but the proper Bostonian still has moments of dyspnea. Maybe it's because along the banks of the Charles air is so rare. Or do you suppose he can't help choking over some of the words he has just enunciated so precisely?

Shortly after our arrival, a colleague of my husband invited us to the Harvard Club for dinner. Innocent as a bluet in May, I sashayed up the first flight of steps and sailed through the massive portal. When the mist on my glasses cleared, I found I was staring at the third button on the white coat of a gentleman's gentleman who undoubtedly had not been born but had sprung middle-aged and rotund from Minerva's head.

"Madame," he boomed, "this is the Harvard Club."

"Yes, I know," I countered brightly, "I'm to meet friends here at six."

"Not here, I'm afraid," he whispered, glancing fearfully over his shoulder into the lounge, where a copy of the *Monitor* had been lowered sufficiently to allow me to be pierced by an icy Back Bay stare.

"But they told me to meet them here," I whispered desperately, expecting momentarily to be sent sprawling onto the pavement. "May I wait somewhere—in the phone booth?"

"I'm afraid not!" he hissed, "Unless you wish to place a call. However if you insist, there *is* a closet."

There was indeed. It had been full when it contained only folded card tables, coat racks, a cricket bat and a leaning tower of glass ash trays. Add me and my pocketbook and it was understandable why there was no bulb in the light socket. There was no room.

For a moment the waters of the Charles seemed to close over me. As the events of my life flashed past my inward eye, along came my last ten years in Vermont in living color and Ethan Allen's words, "The gods of the valleys are not gods in the hills."

I burst out of my bondage, hurtling directly into the unyielding paunch of my captor.

"There must be some mistake," I stated firmly, encouraged by Ethan's hot breath on my neck. "I was distinctly told to meet my friends in the lounge of the Harvard Club at six. Is it possible that there is another lounge?"

"Another lounge?" he repeated, and suddenly this somewhat less-than-heavenly host sang out, "There's the ladies' lounge through the dining room, right above the ladies' entrance."

"Ladies' entrance! Why didn't you tell me?" I laughed.

"Why, Madame, you didn't ask. I thought everyone knew there were two entrances. It's not for me to offer advice on how to enter the Harvard Club."

I wonder if I'll remember to ask St. Peter for the ladies' entrance? Should I tie a crimson string around my finger to remind myself, or shall I take my chances on getting in where the boys are—the Green Mountain Boys?

In the Still of the Night

I WISH I WERE serene instead of good-looking. I'm kidding of course because I'm not good-looking either. The only time I'm called "lovely" is when someone wants something. "Do you suppose your lovely wife would be chairman of the benefit bridge?" or "I'm sure we all want to thank our lovely hostess for opening her home to us today." Opening it? It's never been shut. The reason we weren't robbed when we didn't lock the door is that we took the challenge out of breaking into our house.

I still wish I were serene. I was born twitching and have had relapses ever since. The truth is I'm scared of my shadow on a cloudy day. And at night I'm scared of other people's shadows too. There are some advantages in intermittent apprehension. It wakes you up. Some of my unique glimpses of animals have occurred in the still of the night when a squirt of adrenalin heightened my senses.

This used to happen to me more often when we first lived in the country. There were many nights when George was in New York or Chicago or Washington and our ménage of children and assorted animals was left to my doubtful stewardship.

Something would waken me—the creak of a beam as our old house settled in the cold, a flash of lightning or the inarticulate mumbling of Debbie talking in her sleep. I would get up to check on the children, pausing a minute at their windows and looking out over our moonlit meadows and woods. One spring night with the fragrance of lilacs drifting in the open window, I saw something I could hardly believe in the daylight. It was a fairy ring on our side lawn, only the dancers weren't fairies, they were rabbits. I suppose it was some sort of courtship ritual. At least four rabbits bowed, stamped, sashayed forward and touched noses while I watched in disbelief.

On a cold night in November I heard Debbie stirring and went into her room to cover her up. She seemed perfectly quiet so I stood for a moment at her window looking out over the frost-blackened remains of our vegetable garden. A few corn stalks, twisted, frozen tomato vines and the minature tree shapes of broccoli plants were all that was left of the lush growth of summer. Suddenly the moonlit garden was alive. A rabbit stood on his hind legs, reached up to a broccoli plant and nibbled at the frozen buds. Hardly ten feet behind him a doe pawed the ground with her silver hooves and pulled up an overlooked carrot with her teeth. With the carrot tossed over her head in the moonlight, she was the milk white unicorn of East Indian fables.

Sometimes I've been awakened by the sharp bark of a fox, so unmistakably wild that it made me shiver, although I'm not so much of a chicken that I'm really afraid of a rather distant fox. A fox, hunting by moonlight on a snowy field, presents the whole drama of the balance of nature: tragedy and comedy. He will trot along next to a fence on top of the light, crusty surface of the snow and then suddenly turn abruptly and dive into the snow with nothing showing but his feathery tail, a field mouse that he heard moving deep down in the grass runways under the snow, no doubt. Once I saw a fox get his come-uppance. He trotted a few feet, stopped, right forepaw in air, leapt into the air and dove. But just like a movie run in reverse, he leapt back out and streaked across the meadow in retreat. I have no idea what he encountered under that snow bank. Could it have been sour grapes?

The best late shows in summer in Vermont are the northern lights which I have only seen in Jericho in August. That, too, I discovered through fear. I woke one August night because the room was filled with a pulsing white light. When I looked out through the tiny bubbly-glass window-panes the whole northern sky was ebbing and flooding with waves of pale light that sprayed and streaked and flowed across the sky. No wonder early man thought they were dances of the spirits of the dead. They make late woman feel exactly the same way. They are beautiful but cold, remote and too ephemeral and ghostly to be enjoyed without a large measure of awe.

But the wild white horse galloping silently across the northern sky had an earthly counterpart that quickened my pulse one warm summer night in Jericho. I awoke suddenly thinking that I heard the heavy hoof beats of those handsome Clydesdale horses that pull the Budweiser beer wagons on the television ads. Thump, thump, thump, down our little road they came on massive hooves. I looked out the window and there *were* two enormous Clydesdales, riderless, unharnessed, feathery anklets tossing, trotting ponderously past our house. I had never seen those two horses in our neighborhood; I never saw them again and apparently no one else saw them that night. But their large hoof prints were in the soft earth of the road as well as in my ears all the next day.

Some people get romantic about whippoorwills. I think they confuse them with nightingales. I've never heard a nightingale and in consequence I endow that bird's voice with a lot of exotic foreign charm. But if you have ever had a resident whippoorwill, twenty feet from your house, whom you never see but always hear, he turns out to be a boring bird. One night, toying with the idea of getting up and throwing a rock in the general direction of his repetitious, insistent, loud message, I counted his whippoorwills. There was just time for a gulp of air between each call and that bearded bird repeated "whip-poor-will" two hundred and sixty-eight times without stopping! I have since discovered that neither the bird nor I was really trying for a record that night. Hal Borland has counted five hundred and sixty-four, and quotes John Burroughs as claiming to have heard one whippoorwill repeat his own name thirteen hundred times.

Chicken though I am, a chicken is a larger bird than a whippoorwill and he can't scare me, or can he? There's a strange minor note in his voice. He's invisible, nocturnal and must bode no good. There's no tenderness in his song, no question, no lilt, just a pounding repetition of his claim to his territorial domain. I don't care much for people who are righteously and aggressively positive and I don't like birds who sound that way. Peepers are repetitious and noisy, too, but they are harbingers of spring, full of new life and the assurance that no matter how long the swamps and the swales have been frozen in the deep silent winter, life has been there all the time and now is swelling into a paeon of praise from the throats of thousands of tiny tree toads.

Rites of Spring

FOR TWENTY-TWO years we opened our little white house in Jericho sometime in May or early June on the pretext that the lawn should be cut and the garden planted before the grass in either becomes a problem. The truth is that opening Jericho became a spring ritual, something that purified the spirit and reduced spring fever the way sulphur and molasses were supposed to do a hundred years ago.

The first four years after we bought the hillside farm we still wintered in Manhattan. We would plan a weekend in Jericho about mid-May, hoping that the garden spot was dry enough to rototill and the weather fair for planting. During the next nine years we lived only seventeen miles away in South Burlington and our plans could be a little more elastic. On a sunny day in early May I might drive up alone, vacuum the deepest piles of dead flies and the densest spider-webs, check on whether or not anyone had broken into the house over the winter, pick a few daffodils under the downstairs bedroom window and shake out the faded old mauve-colored scatter rugs. A week or so later, George and I would go up to cut the grass, rototill the garden and get the pump going. All those jobs were in his department, so I gathered up the last of the flies, hung the curtains, and put new paper on the kitchen shelves.

91

When we moved to Massachusetts in 1961, we had again to plan a spring weekend, load the car with the plumbing tools, food, electric blanket and the worn sheets and towels that had been demoted to summer service—such is the power of habit, especially when it is a pleasant habit.

When we lived in Kansas, fifteen hundred miles away from Jericho, we still set off in May to open up the house. Fifteen hundred miles for a weekend? Well, if you work at it hard enough you can justify all sorts of trips. The excuse one year was that Patty was graduating from the University of Vermont and of course we wanted to be there so we might as well open up the house the same weekend. Another year Debbie was graduating from Mt. Holyoke. And after that? Well, any family who will shuttle their animals, including horse, pigs, sheep, chickens and turkeys, back and forth between their summer and winter homes for nine years, will find some reason for justifying the trip.

The truth is that we were called back to Jericho by spring in Vermont. No one who doesn't love Vermont can understand this; and to anyone who does, it is too obvious to need explanation. It's the combination of snow and spring in the air, sharp but thinly sweet, which takes form in the bluets. You really have to see a few patches of bluets each year to sustain you till the next spring; and the lilacs shouldn't bloom at either side of our house with no one there to sniff them and cut big bunches of the heavy, unbelievably-fragrant blossoms. The lilac bushes that now tower over our heads were brought to us by a little lady whose name I never knew. She used to come each summer and sit quietly in the car while her husband fished in our pool. She not only brought the tiny lilac bushes but also a bag of bones to bury under them to give them the extra calcium they crave. I never saw her after that. She may not be alive, but her lilacs are. Every May I think of her gratefully.

What about our three old apple trees across the road? One of them, an eighty-year-old Wealthy, is split down the middle, half of it lying on the ground but still blooming and bearing! And the violets along the path to the brook. Should they bloom unseen? The shadbushes that overhang the waterfall are unremarkable unless you like foamy blossoms over foamy water. And I'm just green-hungry enough in spring to think that the first thrusts of skunk cabbage are the most vibrant green in the spectrum.

The fact is that spring restores my soul and makes me think that anything is not only possible but highly probable. The spring rite of opening the house as always bittersweet. Nothing ever worked quite right or quite predictably. The washing machine balked and almost catapulted down the hillside when we hauled it around back from its winter home in the living room to the spot under the bathroom window where it presided all summer. I didn't tell you about that? Well, we had an old secondhand wringer machine and George built a wooden platform for it. We ran the water into it through a hose struck out of the bathroom window and let the dirty water drain down the hillside. I got a suntan while I flicked the wringer back and forth, disengaging the washcloths that always got stuck in the corners; the aged sheets that I hung out right next to the machine came in smelling of sunlight and clover instead of Tide and Clorox.

Over the winter the curtain rods managed to hide. We were always one short until I found it under the dining room table or behind the piano. What else I found behind the piano each spring might be anything from the tiny skeleton of a mouse to the pair

of goggles everyone accused everyone else of purloining.

The house smelled musty, looked dirty, felt clammy and was totally lacking in charm when we first forced open the door warped by dampness and frost heaves. But after the doors and windows were open, the freshly-washed curtains, faded and cockeyed, were up, the pump chugging in good voice, and the old blue teapot filled with cowslips, the metamorphosis was overwhelming. What fun is there in painting the lily or cleaning a clean house? But bringing an old well-loved house to life again is one of the healing arts.

The Web-Footed Trout Fisherman

SHY AND ELUSIVE as the hermit thrush, he may be glimpsed frequently but fleetingly as he emerges from his metal chrysalis at the edge of Vermont back roads. After a brief period of hovering at the rear of this cocoon, where he stuffs the interstices of his plumage with worms, dry flies and bright metal objects, he slips noiselessly through the lambent birch groves to the nearest stream of flowing water. He follows the mountain brooks from pool to pool, resembling the heron in his ability to stand in the water for long periods of time, motionless except for the occasional blinking of his eyelids or a swift overhead thrust of the long, slender, tapering proboscis attached to his right arm.

His plumage is inconspicuous, usually grey or khaki on the upper part of the body. A rubbery outer layer of olive drab frequently covers the region from feet to mid-portion, making the lower half of this bird hard to distinguish from the hairy-chested lobster fisherman, native to the coast of Maine, or the black-crested firefighter, indigenous to the streets of our major cities. All in this classification are hydrophylic and fish-eating, which, in the case of the black-crested fire fighter is particularly noticeable on Fridays.

The eastern trout fisherman is apt to wander far from his nest. You will very rarely see his mate, though she does in some cases stand guard over the metal chrysalis or hop about among the bushes at the roadside in search of dogtooth violets, sassafras roots, or berries. For the most part, however, these birds. will not be found in pairs. Their mating season seems to be postponed until the pools are empty of fish.

The web-foot is easily disturbed by sudden noise. On one occasion I observed a large male almost submerged in our pool, emitting short frightened squawks. He had obviously been frightened into the deep water by a young Jersey heifer of ours, a family pet who assumed that anyone on our property was an admirer of hers. The trout fisherman, however, is apparently nearsighted in relation to cattle and had mistaken the sex of our friendly little cow. He is also shortsighted when observing pasture gates, being quite clever at opening them but quite unable to close them after him. In contrast, his sight is as keen as the kingfisher's when peering down into the water or out across a pool watching for a fish to surface.

Although he can hear a trout breaking water over the sibilance of the rapids, he has a form of protective deafness which makes shrill cries from his mate or harsh words from the angry owner of the pastures inaudible to him while in this state of grace.

In spite of his deafness to distress signals, he reacts violently to the nearby sound of human voices and vigorously waves off any attempt at communication even when the offending party is only trying to warn him that he is about to back over a waterfall.

The most likely time to observe him is in the early morning when streamers of mist still hover above the brook and the first rays of sunlight catch in the spray and burst into a rainbow. He also may be observed in the hush of a June evening, when he may share the shadowed pool with a doe and twin fawns or compete with the clerical-collared kingfisher for their elusive quarry.

His call, like the whippoorwill's, is never heard until after dark. Silent and secretive by day, by night he pours out his song at the fireside with the same persistence and repetition. There is a certain egocentric quality and monotony in his song which produces ennui in the listener. In camps and summer homes throughout New England he is often referred to as the two-fisted prevaricator. At these times he sheds his retiring manner along with his drab plumage and has been known to attack other members of his species who are not mesmerized by his paeans of self-praise. The Humane Society suggests that a repeated intermittent nodding of the head and the appearance of rapt attention will smooth his ruffled feathers.

Far from becoming extinct, the eastern web-footed trout fisherman seems to be multiplying in spite of his apparent disinterest in females during the fishing season. In addition to reproducing himself, he also persuades others to adopt his plumage and habits. There is some cause for concern that eventually he may outnumber the fish. Efforts are being made throughout the country to step up the production of our fisheries. Buckets of fingerlings are dumped into streams, lakes and man-made ponds. We cannot allow the eastern web-footed trout fisherman to become the red-eyed crestfallen predator, who already may be observed occasionally slinking into the local fish store and emerging with a brown paper parcel which he furtively unwraps and slips into his creel before making a triumphant return to his nest, amid the clamor and vociferous praise of his hungry young.

A Vermonter in
Kansas

WHEN WE ANNOUNCED that we were moving to Kansas City because my husband was to become Dean of the Medical College at the University of Kansas, the reaction of our Boston colleagues was immediate and immoderate.

"Kansas? Good Lord! You mean that scenic spot on the baldpate of the nations?"

One proper Bostonian put it more gently: "Well, it isn't as though you were going to move your furniture!"

"But we *are* going to take our furniture."

"You mean you are going to *live* in Kansas? Oh, I'm *so* sorry, my dear."

The part of Kansas City in which we lived looks almost exactly like the older, more prestigious, residential streets in Brookline, Massachusetts. It was not only the most beautiful residential area I had ever seen, but it was hilly, green, and enormous old trees towered above our third-floor windows. True, the oldest house near us was built in 1836 instead of 1636 (as when we lived in Weston, Massachusetts near the Boston Post Road) or 1763 (as when we lived in South Burlington, Vermont).

But who do you think settled Kansas? The Yankees. The very same young men whose departure from the hillside farms of Vermont a hundred years ago kept the outgoing census higher than

the incoming population in many parts of northern New England. Last summer, in the Historical Society's museum in Montpelier, I saw a display of some of the posters and billboards that encouraged this exodus. One was dated 1880 and it advertised unlimited fertile land in Kansas, special low fares on the railroad, baggage included at no extra charge.

You can, of course, find a cowboy in Kansas City, but you might have to go to the stockyards to do it. I've only seen a few Indians and they wore neither moccasins nor feathers. One was an electrician who rewired our doorbell; the other was a young mother dressed in slacks and a Vera blouse, pushing her papoose in a shopping cart in the supermarket like all the other early Americans.

Vermont, not only as a state of mind or as a tradition but as an exported commodity in the form of Vermonters, is to be found in each state in which we have lived. When we moved to Weston, Massachusetts, our mailman was curious about our mail from Jericho, Vermont, because Jericho was his mother's birthplace.

Our next door neighbor was remodeling a farmhouse in Ludlow, and our daughter's friend's family came from St. Albans. When we lived in New York City, a nurse from New York Hospital used to ride "home" with George when he drove up to Jericho where we spent the summers; and the young man in the apartment across the hall was building a log cabin in Sherburne.

But in Kansas? Yes, of course in Kansas. Who but the hardy Vermonter would have put up with prairie schooners, sod huts and isolated farms in the lean years of homesteading? Vermonters were in the habit of considering earning a living as a challenge rather than a birthright. The grandfather of the wife of the Chancellor of the University of Kansas came to Kansas from Albany (Vermont).

The fact is that Vermont's most significant export has been not marble, turkeys, broken legs or maple syrup but the people who carried the Vermont tradition across the Mississippi. Where do you think Dorothy Canfield Fisher was born? In Lawrence, Kansas, where her father taught at the university and where she lived until she was twelve years old. Of course she summered in Vermont as a child, but doesn't anyone who can arrange his life that way?

In contrast to Missouri, which was largely settled by Southerners and came into the union as a slave state, the early settlers of Kansas were Yankees and Kansas was a free state. You can see New England in the architecture. You can taste it in the food. You can feel it in that typical attitude of independence, freedom to organize their lives as they see fit and a tongue-in-cheek approach toward life in general while maintaining a belief in the dignity of the individual.

Of course we missed the mountains and the fast-running brooks, the flaming maples, and purple shadows on snow-covered hills. Our harbingers of spring were now magnolia and redbud blossoms instead of apple blossoms, and we had a pair of cardinals housekeeping just outside our bedroom window. I missed little turns of phrase such as "I'm out straight today" "such a matter" or "down street." But there were new expressions that were already beginning to sound natural. The radio announcer said it was "ten minutes *till* eleven." The checkout girl at the supermarket greeted me with "Har you today?" and always said, "Will that be all for you?"

when she had rung up my order. I carried my groceries out in a "sack" not a paper bag, and the potatoes in my sack were either red or Idahos, never the square Green Mountain variety we used to plant. But I couldn't miss the people, because they were there. Their fathers or their grandfathers brought coals from the hard maple chunks on their New England hearths and kindled home-fires on farm land where the top soil is sometimes eight feet deep. I have never been more proud or felt closer to the Vermont heritage than I did then, fifteen hundred miles from the Green Mountains, in the heart of America.

On Looking a Gift
House in the Mouth

WE INHERITED a Tudor mansion, not in the usual way through the demise of a rich uncle, but because this house went with the job. My husband had the job and I went with him. The house was given to the Endowment Association of the University of Kansas for the use of the Dean of the Medical College.

Our demi-castle is surrounded by two acres of lawn and an imposing variety of specimen trees. Cedar waxwings nest in the fifty-foot cedars. A redbird couple whistle from the mimosa tree; chipmunks and fox squirrels cavort in the Douglas firs, Colorado spruce, ginko, linden, Russian olive and magnolia trees. Inside the ivy-covered walls there is a thirty-six-foot dining room, built for an 18th-century carved, panelled Georgian dining hall. A Waterford crystal chandelier catches the light and spills a fountain of rainbows from its prisms. There are also a beamed, sunken living room, a den with linenfold doors, a wine closet, a darkroom, two kitchens, an upstairs living room, five bedrooms and eight bathrooms. No, I didn't switch the numbers. Real estate dealers and harassed mothers of ten say it is not possible to have too many bathrooms. Well then, we must have had too few people. When our children were babies we lived in a tiny New York apartment with one bathroom so small that you could reach out of the tub and touch all four walls, though I rarely had the time for that sort of entertainment. When we moved to Kansas our daughters lived fifteen hundred miles away, but we have his and her bathrooms off the master bedroom, and six spares from basement to attic for any itinerants.

The novelty of this house is not limited to the plethora of plumbing. You can't hear the doorbell when you are upstairs (which has advantages during the Girl Scout Cookie season). If you are downstairs, you can't communicate with anyone upstairs except by pressing a buzzer. But how much can you say with buzz unless you learn the Morse code? You *can* talk through the laundry chute. Shortly after we moved in I was loading the washing machine in the cellar when George said something at my elbow. I wheeled around—no George. He was snickering away two floors up on the second-floor landing in diabolical glee, perfectly aware that he had just shortened my life by a couple of years. What you can hear upstairs and downstairs and in my lady's chamber are the pigeons, our own private flock, who live around the chimney pots and forage in the eaves.

If you start down the cellar stairs and flick the wrong switch, the whole house trembles, there is a crescending roar and your skirt flies up over your head because you have turned on the cellar fan, which is just slightly smaller than the propeller of the *Queen Elizabeth*. The fan apparently antedated the air conditioning, and the air conditioning antedated most other air conditioning in the city. We refer to it and the heating as a multiple-choice system. You can find temperatures anywhere from 60 to 85, but they may not be in the room you planned to honor with your presence. The dining room is icy in summer, while the bedroom is sub-tropical. It sounds cool though, because the mechanism is hidden away in the ceiling over the bed.

Another bizarre electrical phenomenon is the doorbell, or should I say the complex of doorbells? I should, because it is. The back doorbell and the side doorbell, when pressed into service, ring one note of the chimes in the kitchen. But the front doorbell sets off the full eight notes of the Westminster chimes. This is awesome enough and really should be followed by an organ processional, but if the button is pushed in rapid succession by a series of arriving guests, it enters into the carnival spirit and doesn't stop playing. This only happens when there is a large gathering; large enough to require the services of a catering establishment whose minions huddle in the kitchen waiting to deck the platters with parsley and slice the barbecued beef brisket. But the wild bells ringing out over and over unnerve them. The first time it happened we thought the button was stuck and rushed to the front door only to find the button in its normal relaxed position. We elbowed our way back through fifty guests and climbed on chairs in the kitchen, trying to disconnect the mechanism. There was no way to do that short of ripping out the whole box, chimes and all. Just as the distraught caterers, with their hands over their ears, were about to not-so-silently fold their food-warmers and steal away, the chimes stopped as mysteriously as they had started.

The next time it happened forty-five ladies from the medical auxiliary were arriving for dessert and coffee. The refreshment committee were lying in wait in the kitchen spraying whipped cream on the strawberry tarts and themselves, when the chimes started another continuous performance. After ten minutes of futile efforts to stop the racket, one of the more intrepid doctors' wives climbed up and unhooked each of the four long chimes as it swung into action. Of course the machinery continued to tick-tick-tick but the little mallets no longer had chimes to hit. Frustrated, the bell system even gave up ticking. Flushed with victory, the daring young woman on the flying step-stool rehung the chimes. After the guests departed I sneaked to the front door and tried the bell. It worked and rang only its allotted eight notes, but the chimes had been rehung in the wrong order so the familiar tune was distorted past recognition. Three electricians made two trips, installed a new button and experimented with accompanying vocal effects until they got it back in tune. They were so pleased with themselves by the time they left that I didn't dare tell them the cure was only temporary. Next day the postman thought he only rang once. But he was wrong. After a ten-minute concert the chimes stopped without human interference. But the window washers who knew the electricians because they all worked at the medical center, could hardly wait to gloat over the fact that the bells were still ringing at our house. The three electricians spent two more days removing part of the front door frame, boring little holes here and there so that they could rewire the entire route from front door to kitchen. It was not my idea. I was embarrassed; they were exhausted. And the result? You guessed it. Oh well, I think I'll just put that old Pennsylvania Dutch sign on the front door just above the knocker, "Bump, the bell don't make good."

The big noises in this house are dramatic and call for some kind of action; the little noises are more subtle. On several occasions when George was out in the evening and I was reading in the den, I heard creaking and the sound of footsteps in the panelled dining room. Having learned from living in the country that the known is less frightening than the unknown, I forced myself to go in and switch on the lights. Of course the room was empty and serene and I felt foolish. I told George about this and he looked at me with one raised eyebrow, implying that I had an overactive imagination. But one night when I was out at a meeting, I returned to find him standing in the middle of the lighted dining room wide-eyed and manic.

"This room talks!" he muttered in disbelief.

"That's what I've been trying to tell you. It's the ghosts of Christmases past."

He had another explanation. The "floating" panelling is not nailed to the walls and it expands and contracts with temperature changes. I prefer the ghost theory, but suspect that some of the "ghosts" in castles may be thermal in origin.

Somewhat less welcome are the bees we have in the walls on the front of the house. Just before we moved in, the front hall and living room were so ominously alive with bees that the men who were doing some painting got twitchy and called in a bee man, who opened up the wall and removed two hundred pounds of honey! A year later while we were back in Vermont on vacation the same thing happened. By the time we returned, the bees and honey were gone and only two rather sticky, plastered-up holes in the upstairs hall wall substantiated the story. The bee man said he had sealed off their entrance and they wouldn't be back. They wouldn't, eh? The first sunny spring day this year they were circling the front door waiting to be cleared for landing. Just before we left for our vacation in came a delegation from the Engineering department of the Medical Center who set up a plastic tent in the upstairs hall. The next day a new bee man and his helper arrived in their netted helmets and reopened the holes in the wall.

"Your bees will never return," they announced after several follow-up trips for smoking, spraying and carrying out an ashcan of dead bees.

I don't believe it for a minute. Next year I'm going to sit right there with my hot biscuits. If we've got bees in our bonnet, I'm going to share in the take.

We moved into the house in August. The lawns were dry and George had been told that there was an underground sprinkler system. Sure enough, he found several round metal sockets on the lawn and a long rod called a key with which to turn on the sprinklers. Swish!!! Instant Versailles on the front lawn, revolving fountains and sprays at the back and down both sides of the driveway. It was beautiful and efficient. In fact it was so efficient that George couldn't turn it off. He waited till the revolving spray was aiming away from him and then frantically tried again to turn the key in the socket. He almost had it, when the spray circled back and drenched him. With the next mighty twist the key broke off in his hand and it seemed likely that we had just become part of Kansas City's pride: the fountains all over town that are not turned off until Thanksgiving. George ran into the cellar and turned off our water valve. The bands of water played on because they are not related to the house water supply. I shouted to him that a workman had told me there was a valve on the side lawn.

"Where?"

"Over there," I pointed to a spot that was now the eye of our little hurricane. George, with his shirt plastered to his back and rivulets running off his nose, climbed down into a six-foot manhole and disappeared. Presto! The monsoon was over. George squished and squelched through the cellar and peeled off his muddy, soggy clothes. I wish I could say that as he scuttled damply up the backstairs he ran smack into a ghost or even a ladies' committee. It would have been funny, but it wouldn't be true. He only encountered me and, oddly enough, only one of us thought it was a fitting and funny baptism for his initiation into a new life.

Manna from Heaven

IT SAYS in the dictionary that manna is spiritual nourishment, but my spirit was somewhat less than nourished by the clearly identifiable flying objects that rained down upon my head when we moved to Kansas.

Kansas wasn't to blame. It was George's convertible which seemed, if not actually to attract, at least not to deflect missiles out of the wild blue yonder. With the early-flowering spring, long, warm summer and extended mild fall, the pleasures of a convertible in that climate were obvious. What was at first not quite so obvious was that a topless car offers no protection from the local flora and fauna. Redbud blossoms, catkins, maple flies and autumn leaves drift down in an effort to fill up the vacuum that nature abhors inside our car. These are fairly benign, and who minds a blossom or two in her hair? I don't share the same enthusiasm for displaced bees or bird-droppings but these have mercifully missed my noggin. What made me more twitchy one summer was a series of near misses by objects of greater density.

I was driving along beside the golf course, dreaming idly of grocery lists and the adventures of our young, when, Poing! A sharp metallic percussion interrupted my reverie. I pulled to the side of the road, got out and walked slowly around the car. There on the rear deck was a nice round dimple, and a few yards behind the car a shiny white golf ball rolled to a stop. Across the fairway a woman and a boy were approaching as fast as their golf carts would allow, their eyes as round as the golf ball and much more apprehensive. We were all so delighted that the dent was on the car and not on me that it turned into a merry little conclave of mutual congratulation. The lady offered to pay to have the dimple removed. I assured her that it wasn't worth repairing, and the boy wandered off muttering, "If that had only gone straight I would have been on the green in two."

A few days later I drove out of our driveway and around the curve where the road crosses Brush Creek. In dry weather the brook flows through a culvert, but with any sudden or violent rainstorm (and all rainstorms in Kansas are both) the road is awash with anywhere from an inch to several feet of water. When the water rises above two or three inches, the local police close the gates on either side and you have to detour to the nearest bridge. But when the flow is shallow, the local residents just drive through the ford slowly to avoid splashing a passing car.

On this morning I should have noticed that the car approaching me was coming at a pretty good clip. I'm sure the two boys in it saw my hatlessness in a convertible as a challenge, because they gunned the motor and passed me in mid-stream. Sloosh! A gallon of muddy water rose like a sheet from their wheels, arced neatly up in the air and drenched the left side of the car and all sides of me. By the time I could blink through my dripping locks and stop to empty out a lapful of ooze, they were out of sight.

For at least a week, not wishing to press my luck, I rode with the top securely in place. But it was summer. In fact it was July 4th, so of course I had the windows open and was going on my appointed rounds when I noticed a clutch of small boys at the same ford in the stream. They had firecrackers, and I kept an eye on them as I approached, mostly because I don't like loud noises and didn't care to be abreast of the explosions. To my utter amazement I saw one boy light a firecracker and toss it directly towards me. I braked suddenly and the firecracker exploded just in front of the car. Several small legs disappeared as fast as a snake's tail through the bushes. Since I had little faith in my ability to catch a guilt-ridden ten-year-old, I continued on my way, drove home, parked the car firmly in the garage and walked around the front of the house where I had been weeding a flower bed earlier that morning. I wondered what that grey thing was doing in the flower bed and to my horror saw that it was a foot-long slate shingle from the tall roof of our Tudor house, embedded six inches in the sod at the exact spot where an hour before I had been kneeling.

So, if you see me driving along with the windows rolled up, a motorcycle helmet on my head and a catcher's mask over my face, kindly look the other way when you smile. I'm not a middle-aged hippie. I'm simply trying to make it to my next birthday.

Apres Ski, Le Deluge

WHATEVER HAPPENED to plain old skiing, or plain young skiing for that matter? Ever get wistful for the days when bindings were strips of flannel worn around a baby's stomach? Anything called "ineffable Golden K's" would have been trout flies and wedeln was something you did in a brook. Skis were made of hickory, pants were all-wool and a yard wide, in two colors, black or navy, and the accepted gear for après ski was one layer less than whatever you wore on the slopes.

Hail the flow of green currency into the valleys as well as the hills of Vermont and Colorado. I just hope the skiers have some left over to spend in the mountains after they've been outfitted on the Rue St. Honoré.

I waged the first losing battle a long time ago when our children decided that Stowe was more chic than the fairway of the local golf club, and that they'd rather be frozen and put away for the winter in the old New England tradition than take another shameful step in square-toed boots. We could read the handwriting on the ski hut wall, so they had to save their baby-sitting money for quilted parkas when their parachute cloth ones became obsolete, and petitioned Santa Claus rather than Providence to come up, or down, with stretch pants. As a result we were able to pay their college expenses. But wait till their children plead for jet trips to Chamonix or Austria, Head skis as soon as they can hold up their heads, and moleskin parkas for $300!

110

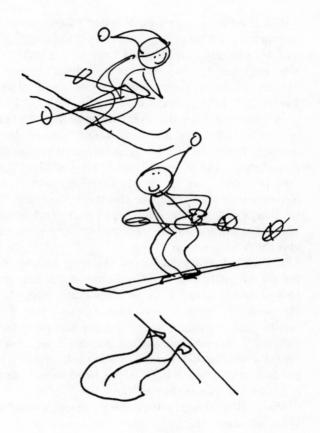

A pox on epoxy for snow bunnies at $250! No wonder they don't ski when they get to the mountains. They can't afford to. They can't even afford to eat. They have to sit motionless at the hearth to keep from burning up any calories they brought with them.

A Finnish (sauna), Bavarian (décor), French (cuisine), **American** (locale) resort claims it is so near to the metropolis that you can beat the snow there. Maybe you don't even need snow anymore. One ad begins, "Once you know what it feels like to ski on Heads . . ." I still think snow is more resilient.

But if either you or your skis don't have automatic transmission another ad soothes, ". . . skis are forgiving." Well, that's nice but not entirely new. My skis have always had to forgive not only my trespasses but my lack of coordination and skill as well. I somehow couldn't feel indebted to a pair of skis that cost me twelve $20 bills. They'd owe *me* something. In fact I would expect them to take me over the moguls with tender loving care no matter what my one head might suggest to the two on the ground. I remember when a ski shop, if you could find one, was a workshop, full of second-hand skis, smelling of wax and leather and presided over by a weathered Scandinavian named Arne. There were other things in the shop, of course, such as skates to be sharpened, gun-cleaning equipment and a lot of dust. Poles and boots hung from the rafters, but they were waiting for spring and the fishing season.

Recently I ventured into a ski shop to buy a wool headband for my daughter and wandered around waiting for a salesgirl, who looked like Rapunzel, to be democratic enough to acknowledge my presence. There was another sales person of dubious gender, but he was entranced with combing his styled locks in front of a full-length mirror. I preferred Rapunzel, but not very much. She found a headband for me, but she produced it with such distaste, holding it at arm's length like a dead mouse, that I thought I'd try to find out what she did like.

She "rally" thought that the emphasis should definitely be on après ski wear. Her suggestion was purple velvet pants at $150, a fuschia Italian V-neck sweater ($100) with a custom-made fur bib ($75 and up) to fill out the sweater. I privately thought a couple of snowballs would fill out her sweater more cheaply, but she "rally" thought this outfit would be terribly amusing. So would my husband. He'd laugh all the way to the poorhouse.

Over her head was a poster advertising "the sun drenched terraces" of the French resorts complete with "exotic drinks, opportunities to refresh your French and German and an intimate approach to their way of life. Eating, drinking, and *le frug* at all hours."

From the picture, which included skis and skiers but no skiers on skis, I gathered that their way of life *was* eating, drinking, *le frug,* and a more intimate approach than I would underwrite for my young.

While she went into a trance over the intricacies of subtracting $1.75 from my $5 bill I thumbed through another slick devoted to skiing and bankruptcy.

"Let Toko do your skiing for you," I read and was inclined to agree. Each year I am more and more willing to let Toko, or Tom, Dick and Harry do it for me. The next page promised skis that take the chatter out of high-speed skiing. I'll admit my skiing isn't high-speed if I can help it, but the few times that I've been carried away, the only chatter I heard came from my teeth.

Another ad suggested the emblem of the crutch as "the perfect 'I told you not to' gift for friends." It hardly seems the perfect opening gambit to an enduring relationship.

Rapunzel counted my change gingerly into my palm and I stashed it away noisily in my Etienne Angner bag, my only accessory with enough status to warrant one more free peek.

On the magazine's last page was a picture of a narrow, golden girl who must have been poured into her golden ski-skin before either had time to harden. She reclined against skis as narrow as she. I think she was glued to them because the whole slim package was tilted at a gravity-defying angle. "The ultimate, wanting your own name engraved on a pair provides character-building self-discipline, in case you have to give up other necessities to buy them." I know what necessity that girl gave up and I wish I had the character-building self-discipline to give it up: *food.*

She was ultimate all right, just a swallow of Tab away from rigor mortis, and I suspect was carried off camera-lashed to the skis. A nice way to go and easier on the weary ski patrol than hoisting Brunhilde on her shield. A jet-set siren to lure the homesick skier towards the Scylla and Charybdis of traction and insolvency.

A far cry from Wilton Shay in Elliott Merrick's book, *Green Mountain Farm,* and equally true of the White Mountains:

"Many and wonderful were the homemade rigs in those early years, and the most wonderful of all belonged to Wilton Shay. On the regular Sunday afternoon ski-bees below the cemetery he'd be whizzing through the trees like an old stager, the tails of his big brother's ulster flapping far behind. He was about four feet high and the coat was three-and-a-half. For ski boots he had old, rubber, knee-length boots with an axe-cut in the toe and a red inner tube patch stuck on. One of his old pine ski points was split half-off, and the tail of the other was laced together with wire. His toe clamps were made of pieces of bent-up band iron, hack-sawed off a wagon body, and his heel straps were nothing but canning jar rubbers. For poles he had two broomsticks with can lids for rings, and as mittens he wore an old pair of socks. He surmounted all this with a French toque and tassel that streamed in the wind when the pack took off, jostling one another down 'Hell Bent Gulch.' They had to go wide-open to keep up with Wilton. From below we were watching one afternoon as he thundered down through, making faultless high-speed turns in rapid succession between the trees. At the bottom he fell. A high school girl slid by, and he began to mutter. Picking himself up, he said to us, 'Cripers! Girls! I can't ski when there's girls around.' "

That's what happened to good old skiing. The girls are around. It isn't the evolution of skis from barrel staves to epoxy that has transformed the old well-wrapped cocoons into butterflies whose only exercise is fluttering near the après ski flame. It's the emergence of she's from the hay and the buffalo robes of sleigh rides to the bright lights on the fashion photographs. But Wilton and other plain old and fancy new skiers are still there. In fact their skiing is better than ever, and on the slopes and trails from Stowe to Sun Valley skill can still beat status down the mountain.

Contrary to Nature

YOU WOULD THINK that the years we spent on the farms in South Burlington and Jericho, living in daily combat, armed truce, or sweet accord with the infinite variety of the Vermont seasons would have taught me acceptance. But acceptance is not part of the Vermont way of life. Vermont didn't accept authority from either New York State or the British Crown two hundred years ago, and most Vermonters don't see sales taxes or federal highways as improvements over the earlier indignities.

> Ah, when to the heart of man
> Was it ever less than a treason
> To go with the drift of things,
> To yield with a grace to reason,
> And bow and accept the end
> Of a love or a season?
>
> FROM "RELUCTANCE" BY ROBERT FROST

I don't welcome the first bright, cold nights in August, the taunting of the first flaming swamp maple; the undulating shadow of a flock of birds in September. I want to shout "Stop!" in October, when the back roads are golden tree tunnels and woodbine and bittersweet wrestle in crimson and orange skirmish around the maple trunks and over the stone walls. I yearn to run all of October backwards like a home movie and watch the wine-dark and flame-bright leaves circle and drift up again and refasten themselves to the twigs.

The first morning, when the brittle fields are silvered and the tomato and squash plants translucent, always comes as a shock, a personal affront. I try to tell myself that the apple trees in our orchard need the long deep cold for a rest period. Well, perhaps they do, but I don't!

Or do I? Would the first chartreuse spike of skunk cabbage be so luminous in mid-summer? The first sharp pings of rain on our rusty tin roof in Jericho sound most welcome after a long drought. I am never aware of the intricate design of trees until their bare branches are silhouetted against an apricot and pale yellow winter sunset. Maybe we can't appreciate a love or a season until it is taken away from us for a while. Maybe the legendary contrariness of the Vermonter works its way up through thaws and frosts, out of the soil like the new crop of rocks every spring in the garden. In the Green Mountains, survival of the fittest means survival of the grittiest.

I like the bite, and in retrospect I enjoyed the struggle. If I parried the first frost by covering the tomato plants and the zinnias every still, clear night it was a personal victory. When it snowed silently, relentlessly, day after day, I shouted with exultation when, after six tries, I maneuvered the truck with a final shimmy up onto the main road. Berrying was a prickly business. Sugaring is always chancy. There is a tightrope walking quality to living in Vermont. You could fall and break your neck, but you will probably step down on to firm ground delighted with your own equilibrium.

It is always a contest: to get down a ski trail, to handle a boat in white water, to raise a garden, to get in the hay; coping with glistening ice, deep blue-shadowed snow, sudden squalls, an early frost or a summer downpour. And so it becomes a personal triumph of the fiercely proud, contrary spirit over a fiercely beautiful, contrary country.

Vermont is
Always with You

I'VE NEVER HAD malaria, but I understand that the protozoa get into your bloodstream and cause recurrent bouts of chills and fever. The same thing is true of my nostalgia for Vermont. Ordinary homesickness would have been more acute at the onset, but I would have recovered from it long ago. It has been twenty-one years since the big yellow moving van with all our worldly goods lumbered out of our drive in South Burlington and headed south for Weston, Massachusetts. Five years in Weston and four years in Kansas City should have diminished the attacks, but a Vermont landscape in an art gallery on 57th Street or a box of Vermont maple candy in a gourmet grocery in Chicago jerks my head around and makes my heart thump, as though I had suddenly recognized an old friend far away from his natural habitat.

What is this magnetic force that some places exert over their sons and daughters, both natural and adopted? Ask a Maine lobsterman who has spent his life wrestling with the sea why he feels bereft when he is out of sight and sound of the ocean and he'll probably say it's in his blood. Transport a city child to the country and he yearns for the sound and smell of the subway and the taxis. I hope all that carbon monoxide is not coursing around in his bloodstream, but the smell of exhaust evokes familiar memories. When I was in college I had a friend from Oklahoma who suffered from claustrophobia in Massachusetts. She felt the hills were closing in on her and that it was pretty sneaky of the country roads to twist around corners so that she couldn't see a clear title ahead. Driving west she felt uneasy until she began to see the red soil, the flat interminable fields and the bobbing oil pumps of Oklahoma. One year in New England was enough for her, and she has lived very happily in Tulsa ever since. But my eyes crave the variety of the northern New England rural landscape; each valley and mountain shaped differently, each village with its distinct personality.

Too many of our cities and suburbs are growing to look exactly alike. Only in the old parts of Boston, New Orleans and Philadelphia do these cities retain their individuality. Every large city is thrusting up shiny new square towers of stone, glass and steel, and one or more of these in each city has a restaurant on top, The Top of the Mark, The Top of the Rock, The Top of the Prue, The Top of Megopolis. All the motels, suburbs and turnpike restaurants look so much alike that you could drive across the country and stay in identical surroundings and eat identical food every night.

They have these motels in Vermont too, but as soon as you leave the turnpike and major highways each turn of the smaller roads presents a unique arrangement of hills, woodlands, mowings and intervales, sprinkled liberally with cows and sugar bushes halfway up the craggy hillsides. The old houses have substance and dignity. They were not prefabricated and thrown together hastily for transient occupancy, only to become the slums of tomorrow. Trees were planted by a man for the shade and sustenance of his grandchildren. My great-great-great-great-grandfather built such a house in Brattleboro more than two hundred years ago. It is still standing, which would not have surprised him a bit. He planned it that way.

When we went back to Vermont each summer we noticed the changes, of course; new houses, new roads, new ski areas, new schools. Most of the changes are good. Abandoned farms have been bought and their dignity jacked up with their sills. Their new owners may be city folks, but they chose Vermont and cherish the heritage of their farm. I can remember, in the Thirties and Forties, when many of these farms were bleak and deserted. Barn

118

roofs sagged and weathered grey houses stared vacantly out of broken windows. Small industries, the ski business and tourism have brought a flow of life and vitality as well as currency to these hills and valleys, and have even brought back some of Vermont's best export: sons and daughters who left the Green Mountains for jobs in the cities.

What we were aware of when we went back and savor in remembrance, when we are far away, are not the changes but the things which have not changed, and which we appreciate even more after a period of living without them. The deer, wreathed in streamers of mist, as they browse on the meadows bordering the Winooski river in Bolton. The phoebe and the whippoorwill, surely the same two birds who identify themselves over and over again, one by day and one by night outside our windows in Jericho. The pine trees that we planted with our own hands ten years ago when they were wispy little plumes, and that now reach up above our up-stretched finger tips; a continuity of life that literally gives us roots in these mountains.

We marvel at the smallness of the New England states. After living in Kansas it came as a delightful surprise one summer to drive across Vermont, New Hampshire, through the White Mountains, across Maine to the ocean and up the coast to Boothbay Harbor, all in one leisurely day! The same distance, although covered in much less time, would only take us halfway across Kansas.

Then one fall we were fortunate to have a week in Vermont in early October at the peak of the massing of the fall colors. We drove through the golden tree tunnels open-mouthed and exclaiming at the crimson swamp maples bordering a pond, lemon-colored birches and flaming sugar maples contrasting with the dark evergreens. Either the fall colors had never been so beautiful, or we had not taken the time to fully enjoy this display when we lived year-round in Vermont.

I have thought since that if I were granted only one day to live I would retrace that drive, zigzagging through northern Vermont, through Peacham and Barnet, up over the hill from Molly's Pond to Cabot, down to Calais and Kent's Corners for a glass of cider with Mrs. Kent and the even greater sustenance of her delicate wit and understanding heart. Then, south to Montpelier and over that handsome stretch of turnpike (which we once had watched them blast out of the granite mountain), north at Waterbury, up through Stowe and Smuggler's Notch, where the little stunted wind-blown trees had already lost their leaves, down the flaming slopes to Jeffersonville and Cambridge, back over the Pleasant Valley road, my favorite road, where Mt. Mansfield curves a long protective arm around one special spot: Frank Corbett's farm on a little knoll at the foot of the mountain. Back through Underhill and the back road to Jericho Center, home to our little house, our brook, our waterfall and pool fringed with closed gentians. A day so filled with color that I could shut my eyes in February in Kansas and see it all again.

But if my last day was not granted in the fall, where would I want to spend it? Arizona in the spring at that brief time when the desert blooms? Hawaii in the winter with pale green water lapping a few feet from rustling palms? Maine in the summer with the warm sun releasing the fragrance from bay and spruce? All wonderful. But, I told you my nostalgia was repetitive. In any season I would choose the same route, the same people and places in Vermont. The delicacy of spring with ice-clear air faintly fragrant with apple blossoms, dandelions spilled over every meadow. The blue and gold days of winter with purple shadows on the snowy hills and a chandelier of icicles at the corner of the house. A summer day with the smell of haying, the distant rumble of thunder, the sweetness of red clover and the taste of fresh corn. These are the fragments that are in my blood and cause the recurrent fever. It is not a malaise, but a warm assurance that comes from savoring the colors and smells, the glimpses and flavors that never fade because Vermont is always with you.

About the Author

You can take the lady out of Vermont but you can't take Vermont out of the lady! Maggie Wolf is a Vermonter by choice rather than by birth, but has one foot wedged firmly in the door by virtue of two Vermont great-grandfathers.

She was born in Montclair, New Jersey, in 1914. After graduation from Mount Holyoke College and the Bank Street College of Education, she taught at the Bank Street Nursery School and at Sarah Lawrence College. Maggie Wolf is the author of five books and regularly contributes articles to popular magazines.

The Wolfs bought their farm in Jericho in 1948 and summered there until 1952 when Dr. George Wolf was appointed dean of the University of Vermont College of Medicine and they became "year round summer folk." Nine years later they moved to Boston for five years and then to Kansas City for four years, but they always returned with their two daughters to Jericho in the summer—even if only for one month.

In 1970 they saw the handwriting on the walls of Jericho and returned to Vermont to live happily ever after. The family census has changed since 1948. Patty is now Mrs. Tage Strōm and lives in Denmark with her Finnish husband and two little boys, Patrick and Peter. Debbie is now Mrs. Stephen Page. She lives in South Burlington, Vermont, with her husband and son Morgan, and teaches at the Flynn School in Burlington.

CHRISTIAN HERALD ASSOCIATION AND ITS MINISTRIES

CHRISTIAN HERALD ASSOCIATION, founded in 1878, publishes The Christian Herald Magazine, one of the leading interdenominational religious monthlies in America. Through its wide circulation, it brings inspiring articles and the latest news of religious developments to many families. From the magazine's pages came the initiative for CHRISTIAN HERALD CHILDREN'S HOME and THE BOWERY MISSION, two individually supported not-for-profit corporations.

CHRISTIAN HERALD CHILDREN'S HOME, established in 1894, is the name for a unique and dynamic ministry to disadvantaged children, offering hope and opportunities which would not otherwise be available for reasons of poverty and neglect. The goal is to develop each child's potential and to demonstrate Christian compassion and understanding to children in need.

Mont Lawn is a permanent camp located in Bushkill, Pennsylvania. It is the focal point of a ministry which provides a healthful "vacation with a purpose" to children who without it would be confined to the streets of the city. Up to 1000 children between the ages of 7 and 11 come to Mont Lawn each year.

Christian Herald Children's Home maintains year-round contact with children by means of an *In-City Youth Ministry*. Central to its philosophy is the belief that only through sustained relationships and demonstrated concern can individual lives be truly enriched. Special emphasis is on individual guidance, spiritual and family counseling and tutoring. This follow-up ministry to inner-city children culminates for many in financial assistance toward higher education and career counseling.

THE BOWERY MISSION, located at 227 Bowery, New York City, has since 1879 been reaching out to the lost men on the Bowery, offering them what could be their last chance to rebuild their lives. Every man is fed, clothed and ministered to. Countless numbers have entered the 90-day residential rehabilitation program at the Bowery Mission. A concentrated ministry of counseling, medical care, nutrition therapy, Bible study and Gospel services awakens a man to spiritual renewal within himself.

These ministries are supported solely by the voluntary contributions of individuals and by legacies and bequests. Contributions are tax deductible. Checks should be made out either to CHRISTIAN HERALD CHILDREN'S HOME or to THE BOWERY MISSION.

Administrative Office: 40 Overlook Drive, Chappaqua, New York 10514
Telephone: (914) 769-9000